Why So Many Sales Hires Fail, Thinking Differently About Salespeople

ISBN 978 1 8383299 0 7

Published by Matt Garman 2020
London, England UK

Author: Matt Garman
Writer: Kerry Parkinson Day

Why So Many Sales Hire Fail

Thinking Differently About Salespeople

Matt Garman

To Dad

Table of Contents

Preface

Why I wrote this book

I've been working in sales for over 30 years and I'm happy to say, I've learned from every mistake I've made and every experience I've had. When I found something that didn't work, I looked at it from all angles and changed to a process that did work. I believe that if you're not always learning and moving forward, then you're not just standing still, you're sliding backwards. This is true for all of us, salespeople or not.

Every time a sales hire fails, there's a ripple effect throughout the business. Management time, sales colleagues' time, customer confidence, loss of productivity, increased workload for the team, a drop in sales contacts and loss of potential conversions.

Nearly every business I've been involved with, has a story of hiring a new person who simply wasn't up to the job. Despite this, most of them make no changes to how they hire when they recruit for a replacement, or to how they welcome their new starter when the replacement comes on board.

The recruitment industry is huge and supports businesses hire and recruit the best talent, in the most effective way. Analysis of their data makes it clear that the cost to business of sales hire failure is enormous. Although financial loss is usually the measure, the actual cost to business is so much more.

Slow or poor onboarding is extremely costly, ineffective and soaks up the time of your management team and top performers while they show a new starter the ropes. Effective, early onboarding allows your new starter to be reasonably independent on day 1 – they can still shadow your top performers, without being a drain on their time or patience.

There has been a lot of research into why so many sales hires fail. The results show that one of the reasons most quoted, is poor onboarding. While this might have been accepted as the cost of doing business in the past, it's critical to address it and not accept it now. As businesses adapt to changes in technology and the speed with which B2B buyers are switching to digital self-service, any outlay, without a recognisable or quick return, must be avoided.

What makes me an expert?

I'm a sales person who became a sales manager, an MD, CEO and business owner. I've been lowest rank commission only new starter in a sales team and I've managed a highly motivated sales team. A critical part of being successful is the desire to keep improving, keep learning, keep going forward. I believe anyone can be an expert if they want it enough. Doing the research and looking into their own practices to see what works and what doesn't. In other words, learning from experience. I've also had the opportunity to learn from the many business leaders, sales managers and sales teams I've mentored from failure to success.

Good onboarding and why it matters

In my experience, this huge period of opportunity is commonly ignored or not considered important. It's always good practice to introduce a new hire to your business products and process, ahead of their first day. You can make a good impression on your new recruit and show them how serious you are about their success in your sales team. Get them started before they join you as soon as they've signed their letter of agreement and while they're serving out their notice. Embed them quickly into your culture and your business, make all appropriate information available to them and include them in general communications to staff.

Early onboarding gives them the luxury of time to absorb what you do, how you do it and what will be expected of them. It gives them the chance to be familiar with your products and services and speak your language ahead of their first day.

Changes in the sales landscape

Whether it's emerging technology that changes customer behaviour, or a trend that has been emerging for a while, suddenly accelerated by an external event, the impact on businesses will be far reaching and affect how target customers are reached.

The traditional B2B model with a salesforce servicing the majority of customers has been struggling for some time. New technology and better access to information, the ability for B2B transactions to be completed by digital self-serve and B2B buyers increasingly comfortable spending thousands of pounds without the need for any interaction with a sales person, has changed the landscape irrevocably. This year, as Covid-19 lockdowns dictated that all business needed to be online or not at all, the trend was accelerated exponentially. Only a few years ago, not many of us would have believed it would be possible to buy a top of the range car worth £80,000 or more, with the click of a mouse.

It is clear that when business gets back to normal, whatever that may look like, everything will have changed. Furloughed staff will return to a different business model with routes to market changed, updated and new ways to contact customers established.

Staff changes will be inevitable as sales teams are reviewed and manipulated to fit the new business model. Good onboarding will be even more important when hiring new salespeople. The new B2B model, with buyers able to satisfy their needs independently, will require any new sales hire to be up to speed with company values, behaviour, products and best practice in the shortest time possible. Businesses won't tolerate waiting months to see a return on their investment and risk their customers learning to do without them. It will be imperative to reinforce value to customers, to offer solutions not readily available without specialist knowledge and build loyalty to retain current market share.

 So how do you organise a new starter to get on board before their first day?

Ideally, you will send them a logon to the system that houses all your processes and company information, after they've signed their letter of acceptance. If you don't have an online platform, then send them all the documented information you have. This helps them learn your best practice way of doing things, your values and beliefs, briefs them about your competitors and provides in depth, current information on your products and services. In fact, everything they would start to absorb on their first day, while coping with the stress of a new job, proving their worth and trying to look like they know what they're doing.

Giving them this head start relieves that pressure. They have time to learn your business in the safety and calm of their own space. No first day stress, no interference, no juggling new personalities and trying to fit in. It gives them a real advantage over regular onboarding that only starts on day one. I call this DMINUS30.

- D = day 1 on the job
- MINUS30 = the thirty days before they start with you

It might not always be 30 days, but it represents the time from them signing their letter of acceptance to day 1. It is up to you to maximise this time and start their onboarding journey, to make sure you reduce their ramp up time. If the person is unwilling to commit to this advance onboarding, it should be taken as a red flag about their attitude and potential misalignment with your company values.

Every business is able to practice good onboarding with a structured plan that includes built in assessments and milestones, however you document your company information and processes. Make sure you provide as much information as you can, in whatever format you have and keep up the communication. On day one, your new sales hire will be confident and ready to be part of your successful sales team, primed with your business information. They'll be self-sufficient, know what's expected of them and understand their role in your business. When you give your new starter the confidence and ability to succeed by giving them the tools they need before they start, you're also giving your top performers support and helping your business to grow.

Now, more than ever before, it's vital to make sure every pound spent is meaningful. There's no economic room for risky behaviour and good onboarding will help ensure every new hire pulls their weight and adds value to your business as quickly as possible.

Chapter 1

Is it time to think differently about salespeople?

Why are there so many sales hire failures? As business owners, we like to think it's them not us because that lets us off the hook. What is the perception of the sales team in your business? Are they seen as a valuable team needed to help the business grow or a self-centred, greedy, undisciplined rabble, only out for themselves, winging it with no training, not following any rules, driven by bonuses, commission and sales targets?

If the perception is wrong, then we need to understand the effect of the overall culture of a business and the impact on individuals in the sales team. The sales person might not fail due to their own shortcomings or lack of skill. They may not fail at all; they may choose to leave to go to a business with a strong, sales for growth culture. A good, smart sales person's tenure in a team will be short lived without this back at base. Good, smart people want to work with good, smart people and they won't tolerate a culture that either supports lazy, untrained people or allows the wider business to operate an 'us and them' mentality.

I am asked regularly if I know any good, enthusiastic salespeople looking for a job. I usually respond that I do, but ask the question: 'Why would they want to work for you?' I'm aware this might sound rude, but it's a serious question to make them think about all the necessary things they need to have in place for the hires to be a success. Salespeople get burned too easily if the business hiring them, is expecting a silver bullet and hangs its hat on one or two new people. Of course, it's quite possible that those one or two people will make the huge difference the business needs, but they equally might not. I can't, in all conscience, participate in this kind of business gambling because I've been a business owner and a sales person, and can see it from both sides. I know how much it matters to both parties if the hire fails.

Common sense and recognising our part in a new sales person's failure will help us to think differently.

It's always harder to question ourselves for our part in a failure, so much easier to blame an individual for their shortcomings. It's true that there are lazy, self-centred, greedy salespeople out there, which is why business owners must know what they want and be clear in their expectations.

Shifting the perception of the lowly sales person needs to be a two-way street, with management and sales team agreed on raising the bar of professionalism. It's very often the case that one or two top performing salespeople are the difference between a business plodding or flying. The under performers in such a team are being 'allowed' to be lazy, they shouldn't be like this, but the management need to act definitively to demand the best results, by implementing a process that illuminates lazy or selfish behaviour and doesn't tolerate it.

Here are a few obvious things to question:

- Did we create a mindset that adversely affected our sales culture?
- Did we acknowledge our sales team is comprised of individuals?
- Did we really understand how individuals respond differently to different situations?
- Did we expect them to know what we wanted without telling them?
- Did they know we value their work, their skill, their experience?
- Was it clear that our culture is a safe place for them to bring their whole self to work?
- Have we been clear with them about the impact of their contribution on our business?

When we take the time to think differently, we might see an entirely opposite picture. Did we let the sales person off the hook? Did we let them take the easy option to be lazy and let a top performer pick up the slack?

Looking at the list above, if you can answer yes to all the suggestions then you can be content that you gave the sales person every opportunity to succeed and the failure is probably due to their shortcomings. I've been a commission only sales person, a lowly paid one, a sales manager and a business owner with a sales team. I have a unique perspective, having seen business from every position and my experience tells me, that if we do things right, if we communicate, if we take the time to support new sales hires, if we don't tolerate lazy and selfish behaviour, failure is the exception, not the rule.

We like to group individuals into teams. We judge teams on their combined results because we think it's the only effective way to achieve what we want. We praise or rebuke the whole team when those results don't meet our expectations, irrespective of individual behaviour. This lets underperformers off the hook and alienates high achievers. Neither of these motivates the individuals in the team.

Thinking differently about salespeople can produce extraordinary results. If you asked a failing sales person why they're failing, you're likely to hear something very different from your assumptions. When there's a parting of ways, it's your business that risks more and loses the most. If you have repeated sales hire failures, you should make it a priority to undertake a review and include:

- How the sales team is perceived in your business, are they considered valuable in growing the business or viewed as greedy, self-centred and only out for themselves?
- How well the sales team works with your other departments
- The motivation for sales and marketing to work together
- Your culture, does your wider business exclude the sales team with an 'us and them' attitude or pander to them? Either of these won't help
- How well you're onboarding your new starters, are you making sure they're equipped with your value propositions, buyer personas, qualification criteria etc?
- Your provision for continuing training and development
- All round communication, is it clear, is it consistent, is it regular?

Taking proper stock of your current processes and how your departments cooperate, will tell you what you need to do, to build a sales growth culture. Changing your mindset will unlock the benefits of a good work culture, motivate staff to achieve results, increase team loyalty and a reduce your staff turnover saving you time, money and resources.

I have met so many businesses that work on the sink or swim mentality. It may be fine for some, but not many. Even the few that it does seem to work for, have a higher-than-average turnover. I think that puts a huge question mark against the sustainability of such an approach. This question is reinforced, because I've met businesses that have absolutely aced the sales culture and team ethic. As a consequence, they have an infinitely more sustainable sales function as well as no shortage of salespeople hoping to join them.

The cost of success

Taking a look at the cost of a salesperson, even a successful one, is a sobering exercise. At the time of writing, the median basic salary for an entry level sales person in the UK is approximately £30,000. Salary alone though is not the only cost you need to consider. It's estimated that recruitment and other onboarding costs – I mean by this, all landed, upfront costs – which is the real cost of a new sales hire, is at least equal to what you're paying in salary.

Landed costs

Factor in all the costs you will incur even before you start the recruitment process. A significant amount of your time will probably be spent reviewing your current staff, deciding what type of person you are looking for and creating or revamping a job description. Bear in mind, that if you outsource the process, or even just a part of it, you'll still need to spend time selecting the recruiter and approving any decisions they make on your behalf. This means a lot of your time and resources will be spent on something that is not your core activity.

When the decision is made, you may have to wait for your new sales person to start which will mean continued pressure on your current sales team, with the likely loss of good prospects and customers.

Providing necessities such as a car, pension contribution, a phone, a laptop, access to software licences, onboarding and any training they need, will bite heavily into your budget and this is before they have the chance to show whether they'll be a success or failure.

Ramp up time

The average ramp up time for your new sales hire to become productive, is often quoted to be up to nine months. This is not profit, or repaying the initial investment in their hiring, this is just until they're making a positive contribution and earning the salary you're paying. They might be selling and achieving their targets by this time, but it will still be a long time before they've proved their worth and you've recouped the cost of their hire. Let's look at an example of what is paid out before any return is seen:

- You've paid out 9 months of salary
- And the equivalent in landed costs
- Lets estimate that has cost £60,000 to date

Salary + pension + car + mobile + laptop + software; this doesn't include your time or lost business

- At the average time of 9 months, they might start to pay their way
- At an upfront cost of £60k
- Selling at a gross margin of 50%
- They would need to have made £120k worth of sales to break even
- Only then would they start to be an asset to your business

Experience has taught me that very few businesses really analyse such investments, or can tolerate this huge outlay and slow claw back of expenditure. Over the last decade, statistics show that the average tenure for a sales person has fallen drastically, with a typical figure now quoted at only 19 months. This equates to 9 months before they pay their way and an expectation of only 10 months, when they might prove to have been worth the outlay.

These stark figures show how critical it is for a business to do everything in their power to reduce ramp up time, particularly as many of these sales hires will fail before the end of year 1.

I think of this as business gambling and highly unsustainable in an increasingly low touch economy. When it's your business taking all the risks, it makes sense to break the cycle. Reducing ramp up time, is the key to reducing risk and is a critical component in getting your new recruits to pay their way quicker, so you can achieve a return on your investment within a reasonable time frame. I believe good onboarding, that starts before your new starter's first day in your business, is the way to accomplish this. When your new sales hire is willing to commit to early onboarding, it clearly demonstrates their positive attitude, commitment to your company and ambition to be a success. Then it's up to you, to make their onboarding comprehensive and accountable.

Clarity and why it matters

I often hear sales managers or business owners' lament: 'I don't understand it all I want is for them to sell, that's why I hired them, why don't they just do it?'

My response is always: If your sales team is not selling, ask yourself:

- What do you want them to sell?
- How do you want them to sell it?
- Who is the target customer?
- What is the benefit to the customer?
- Do they know the value proposition, do you and they really understand it and can they articulate it?

Far too many businesses expect their sales team to sell without the necessary thought, sales planning and training. If you don't provide clarity, your team is likely to go and sell low products at low prices with low margin. This is not selling; it's giving stuff away and accelerates the likelihood of you going broke. Give them the tools to sell, be specific and break it down with basics such as:

- Qualification criteria
- Comprehensive product information
- Evidenced value proposition
- Correct buyer personas
- Proven objection handling set

Without clear communication of these, you're letting your sales team shift the accountability for their failure, to you. Provide value based selling training and have the conversation with them. Give them real examples and make sure they're not mistaking building a relationship with a customer as friendship. If you're hearing:

- I can't sell it for that much
- We need to give a discount

Be very clear with the sales team, the customer is not their friend. The customer is looking for whatever gives them the best deal. Your salespeople must be able to challenge the buyer, find out what they need, explain the solution and why they need it. They must continue to qualify that the customer is ready and able to buy. When this is confirmed, they need to be confident and close the sale. Value training will give them the confidence that cost is not the only driver. It's not their role to decide what the customer can afford or should spend. It is their role to protect your margin and focus on achieving their targets and your growth objectives. Too many salespeople confuse building rapport with being friendly and end up siding with the client, not your business.

As a new sales person I learned this lesson a very hard way. I misunderstood the instruction from a good customer whose operation was based in a dusty warehouse. I was asked to refresh their PC hardware and I assumed they'd want to save money. I didn't ask enough questions, or really listen to what the customer said. I thought every business wanted the cheapest solution and so that's what I assumed he meant when he said he knew I'd look after them. Instead of replacing like with like, that they had been very happy with, I did them the cheapest deal I could and supplied them with cloned PCs. In under a year, these cheaper machines started to break down, due to the dusty environment and I had to face the customer and explain why I'd supplied sub-standard hardware. I had to replace the clones with updated versions of what they'd originally had at cost, twice the work for no profit margin. The toughest lesson for me was knowing that I'd been trusted by the customer and I'd let him down. My job in that relationship was to tell him what he really needed based on my knowledge, create a clear value proposition, ask more questions and not make assumptions about what I thought he could afford. The lessons I learned from that experience were hard and have not lost their sting, even now.

Patterns of behaviour and changing the mindset

Common Sales Onboarding – The New Sales Hire

Before Day 1	Month 1	Month 2	Month 3
Job offer accepted	Nervous	They're too tough	Made my decision
Excitement	Did I make the right decision	Unrealistic expectations	They don't understand me
Silence from new company	Not like I thought	Everyone's too busy to help	I've found something else
Waiting	Not sure its right for me	They don't value me	Hand in my notice
Apprehension	What's the boss like	Resentful	No point coming back in
Have I made the right decision	Not sure if I fit in	Don't provide support	Don't care about team impact
Anxiety	Not sure I like it	Might not stay for long	They didn't help me
	I'll give it a go	No harm looking about	I've left the job

Disrupting negative patterns and changing the mindset is necessary if you're not achieving the success you want, your new sales hires are underperforming or you have a history of failed new hires. Let's take a look at some existing thinking and how to change it.

'Us and Them' mindset affecting culture

When a new starter joins the sales team, they might be welcomed by management but then handed directly over to the sales team to get on with it. Even if there is an onboarding process, the management and other departments won't take any further part in it. The expectation from management is to get the new hire working as quickly as possible, to see a return on their investment. The hiring is done, the new team member is on board and they must fit in and learn the ropes on their first day. The window of opportunity to prove their worth is short for the new starter and expectation is high. If they need any training or coaching, they will find it hard to succeed.

Result: The new starter is launched into the sales team and left to sink or swim. Responsibility for their success or failure is up to them, but the business hasn't done everything possible to help them succeed. They'll be left sitting at their desk waiting for their PC to arrive. The sales manager might suggest that they make a few calls while they're waiting, after all, they've sold stuff before so no need to wait to get logged on, just crack on. The new starter and the sales manager are now likely to feel they've made a terrible mistake and it will be hard to adjust that feeling once it's embedded.

Common Sales Onboarding – The Sales Manager

Before Day 1	Month 1	Month 2	Month 3
· Hope I made the right choice	· No time to spend with them	· Boss is on my back	· No prospects
· Offer letter accepted	· Need to learn on the job	· Behind on our targets	· Basic mistakes daily
· Diarise new recruit's first day	· Need them to step up	· They're too needy	· Progress is slow
· Need to hit they ground running	· Already disappointing	· Don't think they're a good fit	· Making me look bad
· We need to hit target	· Need time I don't have	· Need too much support	· I'm now feeling the heat
· Hope they settle in fast	· I was hoping for more	· Need to get on and close deals	· Figures getting worse
· Will they bring contacts	· They need more training	· Did they lie at interview?	· I'm not happy
· They need to fit in	· Disappointed	· Team now suffering	· They need to go

A different mindset will make sure that after the new starter joins the sales team and is welcomed by management, they will be briefed about what is expected of them and how they are to achieve it. A structured training and development program, covering all the key areas of the business, products and industry is diarised with different management and sales team members acting as the coach or guide for different topics. The new starter is allocated shadow time with experienced team members, to observe interaction with real customers. They are able to ask questions, build their knowledge of company values, vision, mission, products, pricing strategies and how to handle objections. Interaction between the new starter, management personnel, other departments and team members, removes the 'us and them' of a siloed sales team, ensuring they feel part of the whole company. The structured approach leaves nothing to chance and allows for individual differences in personality to emerge. Different speeds and styles of learning can be accommodated to improve results and will highlight training needs

20

very early on. Diarising time for the new recruit to model top performers will give them a good start and remove the possibility that they will learn bad habits from underachievers or be influenced by negative comments.

Result: The new starter is launched into the sales team and sees it as part of the wider company. All departments share the responsibility to ensure the new starter is supported while they acclimatise. Providing structured onboarding and recognising individual differences in learning speed, the new starter is set up to succeed. Whatever the result, everything was done to help them and if the hire fails, it will be clear that the candidate was not the right fit and the learning from that, can be taken into the re-hiring process.

Every sales team is comprised of individuals

In the past, after joining a team a new starter was expected to fit in, subdue any quirks and go along with the majority. The strongest members of the team dictated the culture and everyone submitted to it, even if it made some members uncomfortable. If someone didn't fit in, they would leave sooner or later. It was accepted as a team thing.

Result: The risk of losing innovative team members with potential was high if they weren't a good fit. The strongest personalities and their behaviour set the example. The team would be at risk if any of these 'leaders' left. A less inclusive culture sees a bigger turnover of staff and reduction of the business' ability to attract top talent.

Understanding that a team is a random group of individuals that might only have their work in common, helps to introduce a collaborative culture. Recognising that it's individuals who innovate and create reinforces that it's important not to lose sight of the fact that your sales team is made up of individuals. Some will be just like you; some will be the exact opposite and some might be downright eccentric. It takes all sorts as the saying goes. Expecting disparate personalities to behave uniformly, respond to the same motivation techniques, achieve at the same rate and in the same way is unrealistic. Yes, the team need to reach the targets you set, but that doesn't mean you don't recognise their individuality. Provide a structured process, outline clearly what is required and encourage a collaborative culture, where ideas are valued and diversity matters. Expect your team members to follow your process and invite them to contribute to all aspects of your sales function. It will help those with a low attention span, it'll streamline your path to success and provide continuous improvement as your market changes. A diverse team that feels valued, will offer a rich variety of skills and experience-based knowledge.

Result: Individuals who feel valued are motivated to work harder, achieve more and are more loyal. Staff turnover is lower if your sales team has a structured process, good communication and individual contributions are recognised. You want and need a team that pushes and is hungry for success but they don't all have to be like that. Individuals are motivated by many things and although there will be a few for whom 'show me the money' is the key, it's important to find out what each person wants. Ask them: 'What would success look like at the end of the year for you?' and work backwards with them, creating individual milestones they can visualise.

In one role as a sales manager, I put together a new Account Management strategy, complete with plans for a group of accounts. When I was working on the strategy, I didn't properly engage with enough people at the coalface and when I announced it, it was a disaster. The team's comments clearly showed that I hadn't given sufficient thought to some points and one in particular, none at all. When I reflected on it, I realised that not only had I not considered it, but I probably would also never have even thought about it. It was a hard lesson. The reason we need other people is simply that we're not always right. I needed those comments to show me where I'd got it very wrong. I should have engaged with them properly while building my strategy, but I let my seniority and ego get in the way. If you let this happen, it can be disastrous.

Individuals respond differently to different situations

If a salesperson raises something to their sales manager and they respond with: 'You need to get on with it, this is how we do things. Follow the process and do what you're supposed to do. You're paid to work, not to argue, I don't have time for it, just do it.'

Result: The sales person is likely to feel frustrated and humiliated. If it happens a few times, they might decide there's a personality clash and start looking for a new job. Ultimately, they'll become a sales hire failure.

In this same situation, if the sales manager responds by asking a sales person to outline a particular situation at the sales meeting, it can be discussed, the team's input is considered and a solution can be arrived at. The sales person will feel they were right to raise the issue and feels supported.

Result: Sales person works with renewed motivation and new strategy to deal with the situation. Feels supported and valued, the team is strengthened.

People remember how you made them feel, not necessarily all the words you use. Managers who understand that and use emotion in a positive way make a big difference. Managers with a desk slamming mentality, might get a response, but it will be at the expense of a high attrition rate.

They've got the skills they know what to do

'I'm paying them a lot of money to hit the ground running. They've got the experience I need and I expect them to lift the team and reach the targets easily. I've employed them to be my silver bullet.'

Result: the sales person struggles to get up to speed and find their rhythm, wings it how they've always done, but they don't know, what they don't know and they lose their mojo. When they start to fail, not producing the promised results, disharmony and reduced motivation start to spread in the team. They suspect the new sales super star is earning more than they are and not achieving results. The new sales person doesn't like the feeling of failing and starts to look for a new job. At some point they resign, or they're let go to stem the money being lost on a high salary that's showing no return.

Really, if we're being entirely honest, have we ever had a sales person 'hit the ground running'? I seriously don't believe it. A fluke may make it seem like it, but in my experience its less than 10% of the time. Sales managers need to be up front with this and stop believing the hype around these expressions. They need to be honest with their teams, their own managers and directors and take responsibility for good onboarding, to produce the results they want to see.

We shouldn't expect a new starter to know what we want unless we tell them. It doesn't matter whether they're an experienced sales person, with an impressive CV, commanding a high salary or a novice in their first job. Any new starter with your company needs good onboarding, with their way of learning accommodated. They must understand their accountabilities and what's expected of them. An experienced new starter will usually acclimatise quickly and prosper, their superior skills will help them fit into an established team. The novice will benefit from more nurturing, skills training and practice.

Result: The team is comfortable with the new sales person. The sales person understands the company expectations and the sales process. They are able to find their rhythm and start to achieve their targets easily justifying the cost of their hire.

This reminds me of the image with two perspectives: one person sees an old lady's face and the other sees a young woman. We all see things differently, understand things differently. If we don't provide good process, preferably documented, anything can be open to interpretation.

We need to value their work, their skill, their experience

The new salesperson is under pressure to get results. The sales manager's attitude is uncompromising, they're under pressure to prove they've made a good hire. They make it clear they haven't got time to pander to individual needs. The new hire is experienced, they know the job, they just need to get on and show their worth. The new hire is promised a bonus and commission if they get results. They are under pressure to prove they're worth the money they're being paid.

Result: The new sales person must justify their position and achieve quick results. They are in a new environment, in a new team and their skills and experience may not be a perfect match. If the new team are slow to accept them, if they don't immediately get sales, they'll have one eye on the revolving door looking for a job that's a better fit.

Removing the pressure to get immediate results and implementing an onboarding plan will let the new sales hire approach their targets in a less pressured environment. Diarising reviews and support in the form of one-to-ones will ensure communication is two way and answers any shortcomings in skills, product or company knowledge. The structured process confirms they're in line with company best practice and allows them to add their individual skill and experience to the team. Early recognition of value and appreciation of skills and experience by management and encouraging collaboration across the team, will lead to the new hire being accepted quickly.

Result: Easy acclimatisation, acceptance by the team and reassurance for the sales manager that the right decision has been made. The new hire is given every opportunity to flourish in their new position. They will be motivated, add to the positive team culture and able to prove their worth easily and quickly.

Trust between the employer and employee is critical for salespeople. A lot of the talk of salespeople failing is actually caused by the business failing them. Always do what you said you would do.

The buddy system is ideal for any new starter. The choice of buddy for your new starter is very important, ideally, they are not the manager and they must be a positive influencer.

The buddy will provide support for the new starter during their onboarding and will add an informal knowledge sharing element to the documented process. As an existing member of the sales team, the buddy will be able to guide the new sales hire through their first few weeks or months in their new role. This less formal communication from a peer, gives the new starter the opportunity to offer confidential feedback about how their onboarding process is going and can quickly highlight any changes that are needed. A good buddy relationship will ease transition from new starter to accepted team member. It produces a safe environment and reduces the risk of any miscommunication that might derail the new starter's onboarding journey.

Creating a safe work space and culture

I've heard a lot of businesses say that they don't believe in the idea of a work culture and that they accept other places have it, but it wouldn't work for a sales team who just need to get on with it. The job is to sell and there's no time to sit around discussing how everyone is feeling. The sales team is paid to work, meet their targets and is expected to get on with it and do all that culture stuff in their own time.

Result: Sales staff are under continued pressure to achieve targets, often feeling unsupported. A poor team culture will often be highly competitive, discouraging work friendships, stifling collaboration and will expect the sales team to focus entirely on achieving their individual targets. Diversity is usually less accepted when salespeople are only valued for their ability to achieve targets, in a highly competitive environment. Although in the short-term this can be effective, it's not sustainable. High achievers will be susceptible to better offers from outside, on the lookout for more money and better conditions (culture) or they may simply burn out. Loyalty is not engaged if a person is not valued and only measured by their achievements and a high staff turnover is a likely outcome of this disconnection. Sales managers should never push a sales person's loyalty so far, that they simply stop caring.

Of course, all businesses have a culture, it just might not be the one they want! A good company culture attracts the highest achievers. Money is not the only reward that matters in a high-pressure sales environment. Respect and recognition from the team and support from management, are very important. New ways of working can mean teams are spread geographically with salespeople often home based. Salespeople need to feel valued for who they are and trusted to do the job, even and especially, when they're working remotely. Motivation comes from engaging teams of individuals and recognising that achievements are only part of what a person brings to their work. Loyalty, empathy and recognition of personal skills add to the rich culture of the team and the company. A team of individuals encouraged to collaborate, keep learning, contribute and communicate will feel valued beyond just reaching their targets.

Result: A great team culture values each contribution, with each individual's strengths and weaknesses recognised and accepted. A sustainable, high achieving team will play to the strengths and accommodate weaknesses, provided the attitude and energy is at the right level. The ability to focus resources where they're most needed will produce sustainable results. Good work culture and being valued for the whole self will lead to a stable, high achieving team.

The story that started me thinking differently

I was CEO of an accounting software business and also managing the sales team. I wanted someone to sell accounting software at a higher level. I took on a sales person who had extensive experience even though he was way above my price bracket. He was used to a bigger basic salary than I could afford, but I broke the bank to get him on board. Yes, it was a disaster. I had no documented sales structure and offered no onboarding. I just assumed someone of his experience would just go out and sell. He'd been in the industry so long, it almost seemed insulting to offer onboarding.

I had reservations from the first few days. He wasn't in the office much, but I accepted that he was experienced and knew what he was doing and wouldn't be in the office that much. I thought he was prospecting from home. He needed more marketing support than we had, which was basically none. I hoped that he was going to be the success I needed, but the longer he went with no result, made me realise I had to cut my losses. It cost me a fortune to hire him, pay him for not winning a single lead or real prospect. I let him go and took a good hard look at my part in the failure. I quickly saw that as much as he'd taken me for a ride, I hadn't been clear enough on what I wanted. I hadn't made him accountable or responsible for his results and had allowed him to cost me about £40,000 in seven months. At the time, that amount of money took out almost a whole year's profit. To rub salt in the wound, I found out that he had hardly worked at all in those seven months, but had been on the lookout for a new job. He used the salary I could barely afford to pay him, to tide him over. It was a very, very expensive and humiliating lesson. I learned from it and it never happened again.

Chapter 2

Sales are not where you want them to be, is it time to recruit?

When your sales team isn't performing as you want and your growth is failing to meet targets, you might decide to hire a super sales person to lift your business out of the sales doldrums. Before you take this expensive step there are a few less fiscally risky things to check out first. I have found, more often than not, that the best hires are made when sales are on target and are planned well in advance.

Identify that you do actually need a new sales person

Evaluating the effectiveness of your current sales team mix is a crucial first step. Using a skills audit grid to outline the roles, skills and experience you need, matched to your current staff, will soon reveal what skills you have in your team and pinpoint if you do have a skills gap. If the team have the skills, it could mean a reshuffle, rather than a new hire.

Who is doing what in your Sales Department?

Responsibility	Role 1	Role 2	Role 3	Role 4	Role 5
New business focussed					
Build lists of new prospects					
Make proactive new phone calls					
Maintain CRM with current data					
Book new sales meetings					
Attend 'face to face' new bus. meetings					
Discuss prices with customer					
Provide customer presentations					
Write and create proposals/quotes					
Negotiate and close sales					
Account Management Focussed					
Make proactive Acc. Management calls					
Maintain CRM with current data					
Book Acc. Management meetings					
Attend 'face to face' Account meetings					
Discuss prices with customer					
Provide customer presentations					
Write and create proposals/quotes					
Negotiate and close sales					
Some Other Sales Functions					
Liaise with marketing for campaigns					
Provide accurate sales forecasts					
Accountable for own sales					
Liaising with suppliers					
Organise and coordinate sales meetings					
Lead and run the sales meetings					
Gain referrals from customers					
Attend presentation training					
Coordinate sales training					
Manage day to day Performance					
Coach/develop team members					
Implement sales plans					
Develop the sales strategy					
Own the company sales target					

Part of the skills audit is making sure the sales roles you currently have match your needs. These will depend on the size of your company, your industry, your customers, their buying journey and your channels to market. It's likely that external events and changes in your competitive market will influence the roles you need in your team. Your business may suit an overlap of traditional roles or something completely unique.

 Be very clear what you're hiring for and what you are paying for. Competency and personality profiling can help match candidates to the role. They give an insight into the candidate's behaviour and what they naturally gravitate towards. There's no point hiring a new sales person to work on new business, if their profile indicates it's not their strength, e.g., when you want a person to win new business but they are more experienced in, and suited to, Account Management.

Because recruitment is such a hit and miss venture, it can be tempting to load up junior and senior sales roles with additional responsibilities. It can be effective, but if you're expecting your team to embrace accountability and responsibility, it's vital to make sure you're not pushing them beyond their ability to deliver.

Example 1:

An inhouse sales person, usually engaged in the initial stages of the sales process, is asked to present online to a prospect. They're very good at their current role and it's assumed they'll be ready to take the next step. Unless you're sure they have the skill to present, or you've provided additional training with supervised practice, you're asking them to practice on your live prospects.

Example 2:

You decide to catapult an ambitious junior sales person into more senior sales role. Stretching the role is fiscally very appealing. Paying less, getting more. Unless you're very sure they're ready, you're gambling with real customers who have the potential for lifetime value. Senior sales roles are usually focused on the later stages of the buying journey and should be filled by people with more experience and wider sales skills. The stakes are higher and the responsibility is greater because significant time and money will have been invested in winning the business.

Is recruitment the only way to achieve what you want?

Think about your strategic and long-term goals, over and above reaching your sales and growth targets and align them to your company mission and vision. If you make your objectives realistic, measurable and easy to communicate to your team, the actions you'll need to achieve them will be clear. Depending on what they are, it may not be a new sales person you need. A redesign of the sales team to suit current needs is a far better option and a better long-term strategy than regular recruitment.

Don't rule out the idea of outsourcing elements of the sales process. It might not be your ideal long-term plan, but it can be a valuable interim solution to an immediate challenge. I meet some great businesses who are able to provide well needed support to certain facets of the Sales and Marketing process.

What about internal promotion?

In addition to a sales skills audit, regular performance and development reviews, even informal ones, will help you assess your salespeople individually and as a team. While training is focussed on learning specific product and selling skills, development should be a longer-term process with benefits for the individual, the team and your business. They are most effective when conducted one on one, with a documented record of the discussion, agreed by both attendees. This is a valuable record of progress, attitude and skills, creating a full picture of each person's development for the duration of their employment.

A development review can be used as a career guide, showing a sales person what they have to achieve to be considered ready for promotion. Used as a management tool, they are an accurate guide to where each team member is in their career cycle and their expectations. This will be a great advantage if you decide to juggle roles and responsibilities to meet your sales targets. You may find you can achieve what you want with your existing staff, because you'll have a clear and current picture of your team. As an added bonus, development reviews illuminate any shortcomings or lack of progress and can trigger remedial training, or when to act, if a person is unsuited to their current role.

Development can include formal mentoring and coaching with more experienced colleagues to encourage upskilling and collaboration. The importance of an ongoing plan for your people, shouldn't be underestimated as a motivational tool. It demonstrates your investment in them and shows them how they can progress their career with your business. It's an effective way to build and retain your top sales talent while nurturing the newer members of your sales team.

Still intent on recruiting?

If the answer is yes, this checklist is your safeguard that you're making the best decision. Don't fall into the trap of adding an expensive hire to your sales mix, without resolving these common reasons why a sales team fails to perform as expected:

- Not having the right sales tools
- Not getting things that were promised
- Ever changing commissions
- Reneging on bonuses
- Lack of fairness - people treated differently for no apparent reason

- Looking for better opportunities elsewhere
- Lack of motivation because they don't feel valued
- Lack of engagement with the wider business 'just a sales person'
- Lack of development opportunity

And have you thought about these?

- Is there a current sales person with a great attitude who could step into the new role with more Sales Training?
- If you won't promote them because you still need their role, is it more cost effective with less risk, to promote them and recruit to backfill their current one?
- Are your existing salespeople motivated?
- Have you made your expectations clear?
- Have you communicated the Sales and Marketing Plan effectively?
- Have you set individual and team goals properly aligned to your company vision?
- Do individual KPIs encourage the sales behaviour you want?

When you've ticked all these boxes by reviewing your sales structure and auditing the skill levels in your current team, you'll be in a better position to decide whether or not you need to add a new team member. Your decision should be based on actual data including: individual sales results, attitude and knowing that you have provided the team with all the tools, training and development they need.

Before you hit the button to recruit, be clear about what you expect from a new team member. Understanding and communicating what they need to bring to the team, will increase your ability to achieve the results you want and hire the talent you need.

Whatever your situation, a regular review of your sales team with a skills audit, is the healthy way to ensure your team is skilled, supported, functioning effectively and the right people are thriving in the right roles.

An important lesson for me

An important lesson for me, that I still use in sales workshops, was the debunking of the Sales Super Hero myth.

I'd been influenced by other businesses to try and hire a super hero who would do everything I needed them to do. They'd reach the sales targets with ease while exhibiting a great attitude and being a real asset to my company. The reality was the super hero wasn't so super and sales targets remained unreached. I quickly realised if such a sales super hero existed, they'd be the super hero in in their own business.

After about three failed and very costly sales hires, I knew I had to change my thinking. I wrote down the components of a sale and started focussing on acquiring specialist knowledge for specialist parts of the sale. I would engage lead generation services; I would take a refresher course on needs analysis and I would leverage technical resources to help with more focussed demos. This increased the conversations I was having and the entire sales cycle was faster and more efficient. Rethinking the sales process, focussing on achieving a specific outcome, as opposed to just hiring another person, brought more success and a quicker sales cycle.

Chapter 3

Yes, I need a sales person – recruitment from the beginning

When you've made the decision that you absolutely do need a new sales person and you're ready to begin recruitment, pause and make sure you're clear about the new role and what skills and experience the ideal candidate will need to have.

Creating a well-defined job description can help you avoid wasting valuable time on unsuitable candidates.

Writing a great job description – horses for courses

You never have to start from scratch, because there'll be certain skills and experience that you want every member of your sales team to have. Check your current job descriptions and select the common areas that are needed in the new role. It's a good idea to do a quick search online to pick up current terms for skills, to make sure you're able to attract the best candidates.

Outline key responsibilities with the exact tasks you expect the successful candidate to work on. By separating the skill and experience into 'essential' and 'nice to have' sections, you get the flexibility to hire for a good attitude, while making sure the candidate already has the basic skills and experience for the job. Adopting a 'horses for courses' approach will help you match the right candidate to the right role. If you like a candidate or they're highly recommended, and you overlook your 'essentials' you'll risk hiring the wrong person. This can be an expensive mistake, leading to a sales hire failure e.g., if you want someone to look after your existing customers, but you appoint someone who naturally craves a new deal pursuit, they won't be motivated or fulfilled and you'll soon be on the recruitment drive again.

Setting a skills and experience threshold will help avoid this and get the right person in the right role. The right attitude backed up with an investment in training, is always a better hire than 100% proficiency and a poor attitude.

If the role you're looking to fill is unique to your company or even to your specific product, it's even more important to be clear. The more you can define your requirements to suit your needs, even using a combination of factors from different traditional sales roles, the more likely you are to make a successful hire. If it's in the job description, and you adhere to your skills and experience threshold, you should be able to match any role to a suitable candidate.

Attracting the right candidate

Your company's culture, values and brand, set the style and environment to attract the best candidates. It's worth considering that money is not the only motivator. Showing a great support system for your sales team with good cross company working relationships, regular staff reviews and meetings, open communication and a structured reward and recognition program, all demonstrate the non-financial incentives that make a company truly worth working for. I have yet to meet a successful sales person who is not motivated by reward or recognition, or a combination of both.

Sample Job Description: Sales Executive

To succeed in this role, you will need to be a motivated and be confident generating leads by phone and other appropriate methods. You will have a minimum of three years' sales experience. You will be responsible for researching, sourcing and winning new customers. You must be able to create proposals, deliver a winning pitch, negotiate and close sales successfully to meet your individual targets. You will attend sales meetings with prospective customers and must be comfortable with all levels of management. Previous experience in the industry sector is a bonus.

Key Responsibilities:

- Manage customer inquiries
- Work to deadlines set by clients and the sales team
- Update and maintain the company administration systems
- Maximise sales opportunities
- Communicate effectively and in a timely manner to managers, supervisors, customers, suppliers and other departments
- Present to customers, create proposals, negotiate prices and close sales
- Up sell and cross sell products by promoting the benefits to customers
- Drive for results and work towards targets
- Demonstrate the company's values and behaviour

Essential skills and experience

- Three years minimum successful track record in a business sales environment
- Excellent communication skills both written and verbal
- Self-diary management and appointment booking
- The ability to work in a fast-paced, team-focused environment

- Strong customer focus and ability to connect with customers
- A proactive approach and resilience to overcome customer objections
- Experience working towards targets and success in achieving them
- Confidence managing technology and online sales tools
- Lead generation through proactive research with pre-qualification
- Demonstrated ability to create proposals, negotiate prices and close sales
- Able to work closely with sales and marketing teams and the wider business
- The ability to converse easily with people at all levels in the organisation
- Attention to detail particularly accurate entering of information into the CRM database
- Confident presentation skills
- Superior ability to work in a team

The Successful Candidate will possess the following:

- Minimum of three years' experience in a similar sales role
- Full driving license, no convictions
- Professional, reliable and flexible attitude
- Have GCSE grade A in Maths and English
- Smart appearance
- Business acumen and knowledge of business processes
- Ability to understand and follow company process when negotiating prices
- Professional and courteous manner
- Good attention to detail and an investigative nature
- Self-motivation with high levels of energy and drive
- Confidence and lots of common sense
- Results focus with the ability to work to targets
- Patience and professionalism at all times

The good candidate with something missing

If you want substantial experience, flexibility in the role can add to the difficulty when looking for the perfect candidate. When interviewing, remind yourself why you put items on the essential list, if an otherwise good candidate doesn't have something on the list, remember it was put it there for a good reason and if the candidate doesn't have it, they're not suitable.

In an interview situation, or even reading CVs, it's easy to be swayed by a good recommendation or shared interests. Experience in another company may not be transferable if there are unique and specific requirements. Wear your cynical hat and know that it's easy for candidates to research your company play into your likes and dislikes. It's good to want to build rapport, but it's more important to hire the person with the right skills.

Don't be too cautious when thinking about how to find the right person. Tell your staff you're recruiting, particularly your top performers and the ones with a great attitude. They are likely to mix with other high achievers. Offer incentives for referrals from staff and others, they'll be more likely to encourage good candidates to apply, because they'll be working with them and their reputation will be damaged by a poor suggestion. You'll benefit from hand-picked talent with a good chance of being a successful hire.

Listen to your recruiters

Many people have a negative view of recruiters, perhaps due to their own experience or the industry stereotype. I think they can have a key role in securing good quality sales talent. I've been fortunate to meet and work with professional, thoughtful recruitment personnel. They are the experts in their industry with a current view of the market and a wealth of knowledge and experience. As with any external provider of a service, do your background research, communicate well and be clear about your needs. It's a shame to miss out on all a truly professional recruiter has to offer.

Whichever way you decide to proceed with hiring new staff, inhouse or with a professional recruiter, there are two main approaches to finding the ideal candidate, these are build or buy.

Build

This means developing an inexperienced person (often young) who you're prepared to train. They might need extensive upskilling and have to learn how to use the tools and processes that underpin your sales process. There are many advantages to this approach:

- They are cheaper to hire
- You control the training to develop the skills you want them to have
- They learn your company way, right from the start
- They have no bad habits to overcome

- They are likely to be more flexible in their approach
- There is potential for long term growth and promotion

There are disadvantages too:

- They won't be effective immediately and depending on their ability and skill level you might be looking at months before you see a return on your investment in them
- You will need a structured training program for them and good assessment of progress
- There will be some detrimental impact on your sales team as they will be expected to support, perhaps mentor, a less effective trainee
- This is a longer-term investment and won't have an immediate positive impact on sales growth

Buy

This is when you appoint an experienced sales person from your industry. It is reasonable to expect them to be effective immediately with a quick return on your investment. They will often offer to bring their own sales book of contacts and new clients to your company. I always take this with a hefty pinch of salt, it rarely bears much fruit.

The advantages of this approach:

- They will be quick to achieve sales growth
- You should see an immediate return on your investment
- They will have valuable industry experience and contacts
- And possess confidence and superior selling skills
- Their poise and assurance will generate confidence in customers

The disadvantages.

- Expect to pay a high salary, commensurate with experience
- They will have high expectations of your company infrastructure and processes
- They may not intend to stay with your company for the long term
- Uncertainty of tenure, you may be at risk of losing them to a better offer

- It is likely they will expect a salary increase on results before you're ready or willing to pay it
- There may be a detrimental impact on your sales team with your expensive highflyer causing an imbalance in the team
- Risk taking on someone who has spent a long time in a sector or space, sometimes with minimal results and often failed to impress in a sustainable manner

The other option

The third type of hire is the person who sits between the build and the buy. They will have some experience, maybe not in your industry and they'll have adequate skills but will benefit from additional training. They are closer in profile to the build hire but they will be more confident, should have a proven track record and must be willing to learn

The advantages of this option:

- They are keen to take the next step in their career
- Cheaper than a more experienced industry person but not a novice
- With some training, they can be fully effective in a reasonable time
- They will work hard to fit in with the sales team

The disadvantages:

- They will need training and some mentoring from the sales team
- A delay in the return on your investment
- You will need to provide a structured training process with effective assessment

The key to effective recruitment is always look to hire talent with a positive attitude. It is a good idea to plan ahead and anticipate your needs. Don't wait until a hire is essential to achieving your sales targets because you'll be forced to hire quickly and the hire is likely to be costly and high risk. Using good forecasting and knowing what resources are needed to achieve your objectives will help you to create a stable and well performing sales team. I think it's a really good idea to be in recruitment mode all the time, or at the very least, be known as a business eager to hire the best talent.

Clear selection process

The selection process is as important as qualification of leads and their relationship to making a successful sale. You must have criteria and apply them to every CV or recommendation you get when you're making your shortlist of who you want to interview because it can be very stressful for both interviewer and interviewee.

Imagine getting 100 applications for a single sales position, it wouldn't be feasible to interview them all and it would be impossible to sort out those who will go forward without a clear set of criteria.

It is fairly straightforward to create your list. Using your job description, select the essential skills and add the most important 'nice to haves'. If there is another crucial factor e.g., location or personality trait, that is not in the job description, don't forget to include it. Based on the sample Job Description, your list of criteria might look like this:

- Three years minimum successful track record in a business sales environment
- Excellent communication skills both written and verbal
- Self-diary management and appointment booking
- The ability to work in a fast-paced, team-focused environment
- Strong customer focus and ability to connect with customers
- A proactive approach and resilience to overcome customer objections
- Experience working towards targets and success in achieving them
- Confidence managing technology and online sales tools
- Lead generation through proactive research with pre-qualification
- Demonstrated ability to create proposals, negotiate prices and close sales
- Able to work closely with sales and marketing teams and the wider business
- The ability to converse easily with people at all levels in the organisation
- Attention to detail particularly accurate entering of information into the CRM database
- Confident presentation skills
- Superior ability to work in a team
- Highly positive attitude

These are essential and every candidate must show evidence in their CV that they have these skills. If they don't, even one thing, they should be excluded. In addition, there might be some items on the second list that although not essential, you want them to have. An example might be:

- Full driving license, no convictions
- Professional, reliable and flexible attitude
- Have GCSE grade A in Maths and English

These might not be essential for you or they'd be on your first list, but if you consider good attitude important and won't hire without it, add it to your list. The nice to haves will always include what you expect as standard, but it's better to spell it out and not assume the candidate will understand they're important. If you prefer someone who has some formal education then add that. If they fulfil all the essentials, technically these don't matter because they'd still be qualified to do the job, but they may matter to you and the formation of the ideal team you want to build.

Your interview team, who to include

Whoever is on your interview team, it's important that they are all available for all the candidates to get a consistent rating for each one.

If you have a professional recruiter, they will usually vet the candidates for you and weed out all those who don't meet your criteria. They may even conduct the first round of interviews to save you time. If you've built a good relationship with your recruiter and you're positive they know what you're looking for, this is a great time saver. However, this is an important decision and you might decide to conduct all the interviews with your panel.

The team

The team can be as many people as you want, but it should always include the direct manager of the position. It will be a smoother transition for a successful candidate if they know their manager was involved in their selection. Be aware that a large team in an interview is more intimidating for the candidate and it may be harder to come to a decision with conflicting views. An ideal team might include:

- The big boss
- The potential manager
- The HR representative, the recruiter or a senior sales person

Someone should be nominated to lead the built questions and be the adjudicator in case the team cannot agree on the best candidate. A series of questions should be prepared and asked of each candidate to ensure a fair process. The team should take notes, score answers against the essential criteria and be prepared to argue the case for their preferred candidate.

Questions

All questions should be fair and aimed at getting the information that will allow the team to measure them against the criteria and the other candidates. The team should have the printed questionnaire with space to write their notes. All questions should be clear and unambiguous, that is, not designed to confuse the candidate. They must be justifiable in terms of the work to be undertaken e.g. don't ask a candidate what they think of the Prime Minister unless their role is to prepare briefs for the Prime Minister!

Democratic Decision

Whatever the make-up of the interview team, actual roles should be set aside and a democratic ideal should operate. All team members opinions are equal with one goal: to appoint the best person for the job.

Clarity on Commission, Salary and Bonus

The salary range and general rules about commission and bonus should be part of the job description to manage candidates' expectations. If the candidate asks about commission and bonuses in the interview, the answer should be clear with the company strategy outlined for them without necessarily stating actual amounts.

Your commission plans should show clearly what is needed to achieve each level of commission or bonus. Don't chop and change commission schemes too much because it's important for salespeople to project forward their likely above salary earnings and when they'll receive them. If changes are made it will be perceived as unfair and you risk destabilising the team or worse, your good salespeople leaving.

Money and remuneration are emotive topics in business. It's a trust issue. If you set terms and promised commission or a bonus, you must pay it when the terms are achieved. If it costs you more than you intended, then you must accept your mistake, but learn from it and don't make it again.

Commission plans must be well thought out, or they may cost your business more than they should. Be careful with residual, ongoing commissions because they stimulate comfort and the potential for lazy thinking. An account customer may repeat their order on an annual basis, if you're paying residual commission, that sales person can sit back and get their commission for doing nothing. By all means keep commissions for contracts, but not for historic deals beyond a reasonable period, no more than 12 months is fair in most cases. A base salary is not an attendance allowance it's a salary that is only justified if the person meets the target set. It must be clear to every sales person that the minimum standard has to be achieved before any commission or bonus kicks in for further sales. Commission must be used as an incentive to overperform, not overcompensate them so that they are less likely to pursue new business.

Hiring, firing, my lucky break

Performing a development review can uncover hidden ability and motivation.

I had an account manager who was struggling and I was concerned he wasn't up to the job and I would have to go down the fire and hire route again. At the same time, one of the software consultants, responsible for delivering projects, handed in her notice. She mentioned she'd got a job with a bigger business with a higher salary. During her performance review, she revealed she didn't want to leave because she loved the business, but she needed to earn more money as her family finances had become tight. She had a great attitude, she was a known quantity who liked the business and so, despite her not having any sales experience, I moved her into an account management role. She was trained in sales skills, which she picked up really quickly and she went on to smash every sales target put in front of her. She needed the money and was motivated to prove that I was not wrong in having confidence in her. As an experienced technician, her broader knowledge created great trust in her customers. She knew the products inside out from a delivery perspective. The outcome was a happier, motivated, dedicated staff member, more revenue and a tighter relationship with our customers

Chapter 4

Personal qualities in a sales hire, do they matter?

Yes and no. Your new recruit will have ticked the personality traits that you've specified in your job description. When you interviewed them, they'll have appealed to you in terms of personal suitability and experience which is why you offered them the role. The qualities you want for a new sales hire will depend on the sales role you want to fill. They may include:

- Confidence
- Ambition
- Resilience
- Passion
- Self-motivated
- Patient
- Professional
- Competitive
- Calm in high pressure situations

There is an art to selling and some personality types are definitely more suited to the role. However, sales processes, good sales techniques and sales training are the great leveller, helping anyone with a good attitude to become a skilled and successful sales person. Good sales training is more important than personality or natural ability.

Personality type is often confused with attitude. A new hire with a bad attitude is rarely successful because that attitude may make them resist, or only grudgingly accept any training and it might prevent them implementing the skills they need. Why? Because a bad attitude stops them accepting that they need to do anything differently from how they've always done it.

When a sales person says they have 10 years' experience, do they? Or do they have 1 years' experience that they repeat time and time again, in different companies, without any improvement?

When so many sales hires fail, it is very important to select the right candidate for the right role and the right person for your business. A bad attitude will quickly spread through your sales team and even a robust and supportive culture will suffer.

Do skills and experience matter more than personality?

Again, yes and no. It depends on the role you're filling. A highly skilled and experienced sales person, with a bad attitude, can be very successful in the short term and get the results you want. If you're looking for a short-term sales boost, then skills and experience will take precedence over personality and attitude. If you're looking to build a consistent and sustainable sales team, to grow your company and reputation over the short and long term, then no, skills and experience are not enough on their own.

Building a stable sales team that will deliver consistently good results, with a culture that is aligned with the aims of your business and creates an environment where knowledge and best practice are shared, requires careful selection of every new sales hire. Individual salespeople bring different attributes, experiences, skills and approaches to the team. All your salespeople should be willing to share their insights with the team, in a supportive, collaborative environment. Collaboration helps the team win and helps your business prosper.

A culture in the team that encourages good communication and teamwork will help your new sales hire feel nurtured and supported, especially during their onboarding stage. It could be something as broad as the way the team approaches a particular part of the sales process, or as specific as the way they handle particular client objections. Partnering a more experienced sales person with your new sales hire, provides a masterclass in good selling and is an excellent way to demonstrate proven tactics and strategies with clients. In addition to a good education for your new sales recruit, it will encourage good working relationships in the team. Without this type of interaction, it's easy for a sales team to develop an elitism, that allows experienced and successful salespeople to think they're above the rest. While you might want to celebrate your top salespeople, encouraging elitism at the expense of team spirit is damaging to your company. Your elite salespeople will expect ever increasing remuneration and if they exit your business, they'll take their knowledge and expertise with them. Your new recruit will find it harder to fit in. They will be less supported and less likely to approach the more experienced sales elite for guidance. If a good connection between the new hire and the team is not established quickly, the likelihood of failure increases. Bad for the team and bad for business.

Resilience

Resilience and mental toughness are assets to any sales person. The ability to accept and adapt quickly to change is very important. External factors that throw sales plans into disarray, or technological advances that harm product sales, can happen without warning. Resilience in the sales force will give you the opportunity to take stock, refocus and proceed. Whatever the cause of the disruption to your normal business practice, your sales team will have to adapt very quickly and embrace significant change, if they are to survive and succeed.

What is resilience?

- Recognising the need for change
- Confidence in your ability
- Effective communication
- Mature management of emotional situations
- A cool head in a crisis
- Analysing a situation
- Formulating a realistic solution
- Adapting to a new strategy
- Maximising your strengths, addressing perceived weaknesses
- Ability to keep going after the knockbacks of selling
 - Grit and determination

How can I make sure elitism is not developing?

Protecting the good culture of your sales team is very important. Every good sales person is highly competitive by nature. The killer instinct when applied to sales, helps the sales person to focus and work at the highest standard to win a sale. However, it doesn't take much for the competitive instinct to overcome the urge to collaborate if elitism or ego are allowed to run out of control. If rewards and recognition is based only on sales achieved, top performers will not be willing to share their advantage by sharing their successful sales techniques. This encourages elitism in the sale team, and gives your top salespeople a higher status than the rest of the team.

To protect the team from becoming overly competitive, set KPIs and bonuses to reward and recognise collaboration, sharing best practice and mentoring others in the team. When these behaviours are rewarded, alongside the achievement of sales targets, you are creating an inclusive culture which benefits your entire sales team.

47

Keep communicating your values and beliefs and make it clear what you consider important. Regular analysis of your sales team during sales meetings and development reviews, will help you assess how well they're demonstrating the attitudes and behaviour you want. You might also consider:

- Checking the team is equipped with the necessary skills to sell your products and services
- Spending time with them in field to see how they perform in front of customers
- Regularly listening to calls and conversations to detect any shortcomings or failures
- Inviting feedback on your leadership style
- Regular skills audits and knowledge management reviews covering:

  - Product knowledge
  - Sales skills
  - Attitude
  - Motivation
  - Overall work
  - Personal strengths

Incorporating these elements as part of the normal running of the sales team, demonstrates your investment in them as individuals, going beyond whether they're hitting their numbers. Any training needs discovered can be rectified quickly by factoring them into an ongoing development plan.

If you make these reviews a part of the life of the team and invite feedback, they will be seen as part of their development plan and an opportunity to advance their career not just as a measurement of their performance.

Effort and Work Ethic

Any review, or the introduction of a development plan for a sales person who is simply plain lazy, usually has little effect in reversing their behaviour. I've mentioned the effect of a good attitude in other sections of this book and I believe it's crucial to developing into a successful sales person. If one of your team only works the easiest leads possible, thinks they're God's gift to selling and fails to acknowledge any contribution from other team members, preferring to pump up their own ego, you have a real problem. A common failing in salespeople, one that I see way too frequently, is their lack of ability or desire to prospect for themselves. They prefer to cast the blame on the lack of marketing leads they receive, for any reduction in the sales pipeline.

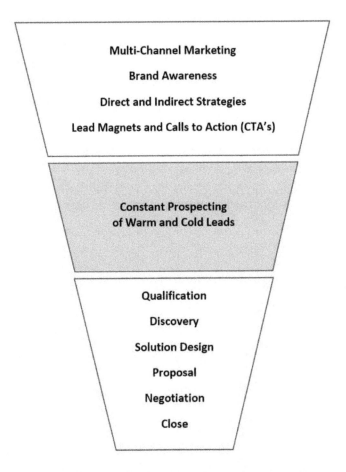

Multi-Channel Marketing

Brand Awareness

Direct and Indirect Strategies

Lead Magnets and Calls to Action (CTA's)

Constant Prospecting
of Warm and Cold Leads

Qualification

Discovery

Solution Design

Proposal

Negotiation

Close

It's a simple fact and needs to be said, unless you have a wonderfully powered marketing engine, capable of producing a constant flow of new enquiries 100% percent of the time, then a sales person who is not capable, or not prepared to generate some of their own leads, expects you to pay them for doing absolutely nothing, some of the time. Lack of effort, poor work ethic, poor attitude, any one of these or worse, all three in the one sales person, will lead to serious problems in your sales team. Even when you do everything right; training, development, good communication and plenty of motivation, you cannot always combat a sales person who has a basic lack of passion for their job. As a business, sometimes you have done all you can and salespeople unfortunately do fail.

When a sales person has a poor work ethic, a poor attitude and doesn't make any effort it's definitely time to cut your losses and learn from the experience when you recruit for their replacement.

Willingness to commit to continuous improvement

Of all the attributes you might want your new recruit to have, a willingness to commit to continuous improvement is the most important. They must show by their attitude and experience that they are open to new ideas and able to accept change, however often and rapidly it comes. If they're not committed to continuous improvement they are, if effect, moving backwards and will get left behind. If they're unable to adapt to rapid change, technological advances and external events, they will be a liability, an anchor holding your sales team back, as your business adapts to different needs and improves the way you do business.

Chapter 5

Induction, Onboarding and Training

Anyone starting a new job needs to learn the ropes in their new company. Even the most experienced and skilled person needs to know how to apply their skills and talent in a new environment. They need to know exactly what's expected of them and how they are to achieve it.

Any new hire is a substantial investment in time and resources. Salespeople who are process driven, with the skills, habits and behaviour needed might seem a safer option, but salespeople with the right attitude will be open to learning the specifics of the company's products and services and the differences in the sales process in the industry. A sales person with a positive attitude and plenty of energy, in a company with a structured onboarding process, will outperform a more experienced sales person without any formal induction.

I think it's important to imagine what your new recruit will tell their nearest and dearest about their first day in your company. We all know the first day in new job is a big deal, full of anticipation, hope and anxiety. It's vital to make it positive, because everyone who knows your new hire will ask them how it went and what your company is like. I tell audiences that you want them feeling happy and sad – happy that they're really found the right role but sad because they've got to wait until tomorrow to get back at it (although I admit the sad part is wishful thinking!).

How Does Good Onboarding Make a Difference?

Good onboarding is the difference between setting a new starter up for success or letting them fail. However experienced, however skilled your sales person is, effective onboarding is essential for every new hire because your company is unique.

Everything your company does will be slightly different from where they've been before. Your processes, your terminology, your products, your values and your culture. Their sales experience will help them with customers, but they're not ready to represent your company, until they know who you are, what you do and how you do it.

Providing a structured programme that covers all the key areas of your business, products, company values and goals will help them settle in quickly. Investing this time shows you value and support them and provides significant benefits:

- New hire fits into the team quickly, with confidence
- The team sees the new hire getting up to speed with accountability and responsibility
- The business sees a quicker return on investment with reduced ramp up time
- Risk of a sales hire failure is minimised

Sales is Sales – so what's to learn?

Sales *is* sales and that's why you asked for experience in your job description. The art of selling is in the attitude and personality of your salespeople and what they bring to the role. The science, and what you need for sustainable sales success, is your unique company information underpinned by a documented sales strategy. That's where the learning comes in. Yes, an experienced sales person knows about value proposition, target customers, elevator pitch, company mission, sales process, handling objections and how to make a winning pitch, but their experience is likely to be honed for their last company, not for yours. Your company information, your way of doing everything is unique and they need to learn it, as quickly as possible.

Whether they have years of experience in your industry or they're a brand-new sales person in their first role, they need structured onboarding with measures and assessment of progress to learn about your company.

You could just tell them to read a brochure or two and look at the website thinking they'll learn as they work, but letting a sales person practice on live customers doesn't make any sense and is not good business practice. It's a hope outweighing common-sense approach, that will put more strain on your existing sales team, might see prospects burned by a generic approach that doesn't answer specific requirements and may harm your reputation. Comprehensive onboarding, with checks and balances, is the most effective and cost-effective way to ensure your new starter is representing your company the way you want them to, while quickly becoming a valuable member of your sales team.

Onboarding

If you don't already have a structured onboarding program, develop one. It will give you a blueprint that you can adjust to be relevant for your new starter's role and save you a fortune in the long term. All new staff need good induction to help them to be effective as easily and quickly as possible, whatever their position. Include the items that are most important to you, these might be:

- Your company vision
- Value proposition and your products' value to clients
- Your sales process specific to your products/services
- Who your competition is?
- Who your target customers are and where to find them?

- Your channels to market
- Your terminology – getting your new hire speaking your company language

Make sure your expectations are clear:

- Show how their performance will be evaluated
- Set out targets and timeframes for achievement

Creating a comprehensive sales onboarding plan for the induction and mobilisation of a new sales recruit is a checklist for you and for them to refer to. The plan should be designed to be a transparent, working document. The starting point as they progress, charting their targets and highlighting any shortcomings. You'll quickly see if they're meeting your expectations and requirements and so will they. This clarity allows you to initiate additional training if required and helps them manage their learning process with no surprises. An essential part of their learning is your documented best practice. Whatever your industry, size of company or operating practices, a Sales Playbook will help your new starter understand your best practice and is the go-to for every customer scenario they're likely to face. It's a very valuable part of their onboarding process.

The Sales Playbook

Your Sales Playbook is the home for your documented processes and is built around selling your product, to your specific customer base, sales DNA and IP. Analysing your sales information to show how you achieve successful customer conversions and identify how your best salespeople operate will capture your best practice.

Whether it's a digital or paper document your playbook should include:

- Information on your company's identity and beliefs
- Your value proposition
- Your product offering
- Your pricing strategy
- Information on the market in which you operate
- Guide salespeople through all the stages of the process of converting a lead
- Document the sales process and methodology
- Be clear about who is responsible for each stage of the process
- Show how technology is used within the process - effective CRM use is the starting point but there are many other pieces of software available to streamline the lead conversion process
- Best practice – institutionalising what your best salespeople are already doing e.g. objection handling
- Identify the best responses to repeated issues raised by customers, incorporate them into the playbook
- Document key behaviour for all stages of the sales process to enable use of the combined knowledge base in your business

- Include a guide to all key sales and marketing collateral
- Templates for pitches, proposals, ROI calculators and other materials for client interaction

To be truly useful, your playbook must reflect what is really happening day-to-day in your sales team. It must be based on real data and customer information, not reports from your sales managers or Sales Directors. If your sales process is not documented, I recommend taking the time to deconstruct it, based on your most successful sales and make it available to your sales team.

Your playbook must be practical, regularly updated and use real experience from your company. It must be viewed as a living entity that constantly evolves and develops, to keep you ahead of the competition. It should be introduced to employees during their induction process and used by all staff to achieve consistent results.

At the end of the onboarding program, your new starter should understand your company goals and their own role in helping to achieve them. If you include skills training and practice elements (e.g., role-playing) it is worthwhile continuing these beyond the induction process.

An example onboarding plan:

SALES ENABLA — Sales Onboarding and Reboarding	DMINUS30 (countdown)	Week 1	Month 1	Month 2	Month 3
General HR	Complete HR process, sign Contract of Employment and get basic joining details arranged	Welcome drinks Walk round induction Technology induction	TBC	TBC	TBC
Coach/Buddy	Telephone introductions to Buddy, build rapport	Buddy meets new hire Lunch/get together with Sales/Marketing team	New Hire shadows Buddy activity Daily interactions Open conversations	Daily interactions Weekly summary	Daily interactions Weekly summary
Sales Playbook	Access to Sales Playbook Login sent with Job Offer Review Playbook content	Present Playbook to Buddy to demonstrate that New Hire understands Playbook	Reference Playbook in daily calls and activity with Buddy	Using Playbook to reinforce all learnings	Making Playbook content part of all sales activities
Training	Learning has already started through the Manual and remote tools that are used	Discuss development plan in line with objectives and targets for NH	Review of Week 1 learnings, discuss improvements and weekly/monthly objectives	Review of Month 1 learnings, discuss improvements for Month 2 and update plan if needed	Review of Month 2 learnings, discuss improvements for Month 3 and update plan
Activity	Digestion of Sales Knowledge and possible Assessment	Mostly shadowing Buddy	Mostly shadowing Buddy W = No of Contacts/Calls X = No of Meetings Sat Y = Value of Quotes	W = No of Contacts/Calls X = No of Meetings Sat Y = Value of Quotes	W = No of Contacts/Calls X = No of Meetings Sat Y = Value of Quotes Z = Value of Orders
Performance	Discuss performance levels in conceptual terms with Buddy	Buddy and New Hire agree performance targets Focus on accountability	Review activity levels Adjust activity if needed	Review Month 1 performance levels and adjust if needed	Review Month 2 performance levels and adjust if needed

Opportunity   Danger Zone (when the salespeople are at greatest risk of failing)

Days 1-7 are at the granular level, focussing on detail and setting up the next three months. Lay out weeks 1-4 with assessment guides and targets linked to activities. Although a 90 day onboarding plan should be long enough, setting out a schedule for six months is valuable for the employee and for you to know how they're tracking after the intensive focus of the onboarding three months has finished.

An approach like this, with expecations, goals and objectives clearly set out, allows a new employee to transition smoothly into the company and helps them succeed. At any stage it will be clear how they are fitting in, whether they are meeting expectations and if they need any remedial action.

If they struggle from day one and continue without improving, you will know quickly and can act before too much damage is done to your sales team morale or your company's reputation.

Starting the journey before day one

Good onboarding is a lengthy process and needs commitment from the sales manager and the right attitude from the new starter. It's not uncommon for managers to think: 'I did it the hard way and so will you' or for the new starter to think: 'I don't need systems and processes, I don't need support, I know what I'm doing, I have the experience and skill'. A different mindset is needed and both sales manager and new hire must recognise the value of your onboarding process. Some salespeople, including sales managers, rarely train or learn new skills once they think they have reached a certain standard. I have never come away from a sales training session or from reading a book about business without thinking:

- I've learned something new
- I need to change X or Y
- I've been doing too much of something
- I haven't been doing enough of something

In other words, all training is valuable even if just a refresher for a very experienced sales person. During onboarding, it's not only a refresher, but also learning your company's way, your best practice and how you want every one of your sales team to communicate with your customers.

The time spent on onboarding is valuable and essential, if you want to see a good return on the investment you've made in your new sales hire. But reducing the onboarding time is logical and practical. Which is why you need to start the process as soon as they've signed their letter of agreement. They should be keen to know as much as possible, as soon as possible (you know this because good attitude was one of your essentials, right?). Even if they're working out their notice at their old job you can start including them in appropriate correspondence. In some cases, a person will be on 'gardening' leave, particularly if they are coming from a competitor which puts them in a great position to have a lot of what they need to know from Day 1.

DMINUS30

DMINUS30 is Day 1 minus 30 days. Start introducing your new hire to their manager and the sales team, face to face or online and give them their onboarding plan. Early assessment of skills and starting product training will give them a great start and reduce ramp up time considerably.

Key advantages of **DMINUS30**:

- New hire is set up for success with company knowledge 30 Days before their first day
- Ready to go on their first day on the job, primed with your key sales information and best practice
- Faster return on your investment
- Risk of failure significantly reduced
- They'll be on brand, on message, on target
- Real progress measured from Day 1, no first day excuses
- Faster achievement of the standard you want
- Self-sufficient from Day 1
- Eliminates baby-sitting that reduces productive sales time for your top performers
- Accountability and responsibility from first day

Although selling can be complex (with some salespeople trying to make it too complex), too few businesses are willing to instil a discipline of wanting to improve, or create a best practice blue print. This is often attributed to lack of time and the need to achieve short term goals. Good onboarding is the most effective way to instil a culture of best practice and continuous improvement. It sets the expectation of accountability, training for skills and showing the value of transparent process from Day 1. When external pressure is a critical factor threatening business success, good process and skills practice, will help the sales team ramp up their effort to produce consistent results, that are more likely to meet short- and long-term targets.

I've lost count of the number of sales and business leaders I've met, who said they'd thought everything was all set for their new hire to start on a specific date, only to have the person simply not turn up. The cost of this failure to show up, is enormous in every way. The risk can be reduced by implementing a DMINUS30 strategy. The chance of a no-show is significantly reduced when a relationship with the new hire is already in progress. There is investment from the new starter and it provides an incomparable opportunity to set the scene for a great hire. Lost management time, money spent on the recruitment process, losing face in front of the team along with the knock-on internal challenges that led to wanting to hire a new sales person in the first place.

Chapter 6

Importance of good communication

How you communicate matters as much as what is communicated. We all imagine we're good communicators because we've been doing it all our lives. We assume the person listening to us is hearing what we intend them to hear, but this is not necessarily true.

Good communication isn't just about sharing information or you talking. In the broadest sense, it's using every method available to start a conversation with your staff, your customers and future customers. Communication is a two-way interaction: delivering a message and knowing it's been understood.

The expression 'gift of the gab' is rarely used as a compliment and it's mostly aimed at salespeople, but having a natural gift for conversation *is* a gift. It makes asking questions and developing a genuine connection easy and fulfilling for both people. The communication techniques used with a customer to make sure they want to do business with you, should also be used to get to know your new starter.

Your communication style has verbal and non-verbal components. These are equally important in delivering your message. Non-verbal components include:

- Body language
- Gestures
- Clothing
- Behaviour
- Eye contact

In addition to these, tone of voice indicates how you feel, smiling or frowning will colour what you say and even your choice of words will add a layer of meaning that you may or may not intend.

Acknowledging a difference in status in a conversation is vital because what you say and how you say it will be received very differently if a person reports to you, or you to them, or you're equals. It's always important to check that your message is being received and understood in the way you mean it to be, it's easily done by asking the question: 'Is that ok - have I made it clear?' If you're not confident in your verbal communication, then write it down. It's good practice to follow up any face-to-face communication with customers, staff or management with written confirmation of what was discussed and agreed. This makes sure your message was received properly and gives them the opportunity to say if there is any misunderstanding or miscommunication.

Building a good relationship

Knowing how to build a good relationship is an essential skill that should be included in any sales training. How well we are able to do it, depends on personality, life experience and practice.

As soon as your new starter accepts the position with you, they will start to learn and judge the culture, values and beliefs of your company by how and what you communicate.

The time between the letter of acceptance and the official start date is a crucial time to introduce your new recruit to their manager, their team and your company information. If your new starter is working out their notice or on gardening leave, before day one with you, they should be encouraged to start engaging and thinking about their new role. Regular contact, by phone, email, video call and in person, will start to build the relationship with your company.

It will also help you assesses their communication skills, giving you invaluable insight and advance warning of any shortfall, allowing you to make sure these are included in the onboarding schedule.

Early assessment and remedial training of these 'soft' sales skills will ensure your new starter is ready to interact with your customers and represent your company as soon as possible.

What helps you communicate well?

- **Good body language.** We pick up clues about a person from their body language, even if we're unaware we're doing it. We know instinctively when they say one thing but mean another. Imagine a person making eye contact, sitting or standing properly and using relaxed, controlled hand gestures. Now imagine someone looking away, leaning on the wall or slouching in a chair, idly tapping their leg while speaking. Even if they said the same thing, we would hear a very different message. You don't have to be an expert at reading body language, just be aware of what non-verbal message you're sending and by the other person's body language, what they're hearing. It's very important not to send out unintended signals or miss signals that are being sent to you.

- **Tone of voice.** Understanding how the volume, pitch and speed at which we talk affects the listener can make the difference between the message being heard or rejected. Whether you choose simple or complex words, it's usually the tone of voice that makes the difference between feeling lectured to, or being involved in a conversation. Again, the clues are there for you to pick up. You can match your tone, speed and volume to theirs. If they speak loudly, you should make sure your volume level is comfortable for them. The same with their pace. If they speak slowly, you should too. It may indicate they like time to consider and if you pick up the pace you will make them uncomfortable and they will lose interest in what you're saying.

- **Empathy.** Ability to be empathetic varies wildly from person to person and in different situations, we sometimes are less empathetic than usual. This is often the case with a new starter due to the power balance of the relationship. You're paying them, they need to step up. While this is understandable, it won't always produce the best result. It's always a good idea to hear and understand your new starter's point of view, especially in the early days of building the relationship. Connecting at several levels: as a boss, as a mentor, as another person wanting the same goal (success) requires both parties to be willing to find a level trust and empathy to make the relationship work effectively. It's not enough to say: 'I'm the boss, do this.'

- **Understand when they're holding back.** This is picking up non-verbal clues and practising active listening. A new starter might not have revealed some things about their training or skills that you need to know. If you're listening properly, you'll be able to pick this up in their body language and careful answers. They may not be that important but any reticence should be followed up just in case.

- **Speak plainly, using evidence and examples.** Your new starter will be much better equipped if you speak in normal language and use actual examples to illustrate what you mean. It's not necessary to impress them with fancy words and catchy phrases, they need to know how you want them to be effective as quickly as possible.

- **Be interested.** They may only be a very junior sales recruit but it will make the communication easier, the relationship better and increase their motivation if you're actually interested in who they are and what they say.

If you're not really that interested because you're too busy and just want them to do the job, that's totally understandable, but think about handing them on (all same bullet) to someone who will be and has the time. It will pay dividends in terms of loyalty and engagement.

- **Face value**. Hear what they say and take it at face value. Try not to read complicated motivations into simple statements. Sometimes when they say: 'I'm well' when you ask: 'How are you?' is just a statement of fact, not them trying to cover up some deadly killer disease they don't want to talk about!

- **Understanding.** Don't necessarily assume they are taking in everything you're saying. Your new starter might be reluctant to ask you to repeat something or ask for clarification. Be alert to any hesitation. It's a good idea to ask a few questions to make sure they're following and understand what you mean.

Inclusive behaviour

Inclusive behaviour is much more than a quick shared birthday cake once in a while. It means each employee knowing they are safe to bring their whole self to work, that diversity is accepted and different opinions are respected.

It should start with onboarding and continue into the work community. An inclusive culture allows all employees to feel connected to the company, to their teams and to each other.

Research has been shown that an inclusive workplace allows staff to be innovative, achieve financial goals more easily and are less likely to leave in their first year. It makes sense that better engagement, a feeling of well-being and being valued by your company will lead to more sustainable success.

I've noticed that in most of my interaction with sales teams, praise is not often spoken about. Most of the talk is around hitting the monthly sales targets. I like to remind sales managers not to forget the impact of a simple 'Thank You' at the right moment. We don't always remember the actual words used, but we do remember how we felt. This is true for both good and bad experiences. In the past, I didn't focus on celebrating success nearly enough. I've learned over time, that it's one of the few times everyone can feel good together and it helps to feed the positivity pot.

How do you create an inclusive workplace?

- **Encourage cooperation.** Ask your staff to help each other. Expect them to work as a team, aiming for the same goal. Try to avoid overly competitive behaviour in the race to be the best, because it prevents sharing. The sales team environment can be highly competitive and it's natural to want to win. Unfortunately, greed and selfishness can be part of being the top dog, characteristics that have never been particularly endearing in anyone. Highlighting each person's role in closing a sale or reaching a target and encouraging a concept of, if one wins, we all win, will discourage these. Greed and selfishness have no place in a professional sales team.

- **Collaboration.** To get the best out of all the team, encouraging collaboration shares ideas, skills and experience. Ask the team in meetings what they think, keep the conversation going to demonstrate that it's safe to have an opposing view. Always give credit to a person with a good idea or contribution. If you allow ideas to become 'company' ideas without due credit given, you will start to erode confidence in the inclusiveness of the workplace and the ideas will dry up or be kept for the next employer.

- **Communication.** Good communication, the two-way street, with freedom to speak both up and down the organisational structure ensures all employees feel valued.

- **Proper access to sales tools.** Make sure every person has access to and training in, the sales tools they need to help them be effective and efficient in their role. I've lost count of the number of times I've been presented with sales collateral that is several versions or even years out of date. Make sure everything available to your team is current and relevant.

- **Preparation and advance information for meetings.** Diarise meetings in plenty of time, send an agenda, be clear about what preparation is expected for the meeting. Don't spring surprises on attendees, make sure everyone is ready to do their best and contribute as fully as possible.

- **Employee surveys, informal feedback.** Send regular surveys to staff to ask how they're feeling about the workplace. Feedback may be uncomfortable, but it's important for the company's success, to find out how the workforce is feeling. Employees who feel their opinions matter and can contribute to decisions that affect their work will feel connected to the success of the company. Informal chats over coffee or in the office lunch room will help everyone feel part of a concerted effort to make things better. No subject should seem off limits and the feedback loop should always be open.

- **Training and development.** Good training and development should be available for all staff on an ongoing basis, especially if you have new technology or systems. Your budget for new software must include staff training and rollout to ensure the technology works for you. Your employees need to have one-on-one development reviews to know that there is opportunity for advancement in the company. Make sure part of your assessment is recognition of their skill and that their individual perspective is valued. Without a clear view of career progression, their growth will be limited and they may even start looking for advancement outside your company. If your budget doesn't stretch to funding for further study it can be enough to offer time or simple encouragement to support an employee's self-funded education.

 I've seen a huge disparity in the age of salespeople. Their experience, knowledge, methods of consuming information and expectations when joining a new company. It's important to understand how training methods have shifted over the last 30-40 years. Many businesses went from having in-house training teams, to outsourcing all their needs, dropping back to no training at all. There is a gradual shift back to inhouse training as the need to be competitive and consistent becomes more urgent. Part of the onboarding conversation should be to understand the most effective methods of training for an individual. It really doesn't matter which is used, but it is critical that it suits the person's way of consuming information. If you don't believe or see the value, in ongoing training, ask yourself how your salespeople are honing their skills. The cold, hard fact is, that if you're not investing in training, they're learning on the job. You don't want them practising on the prospects, that you've probably spent hundreds, if not thousands, of pounds for them to get in front of.

- **Keeping the conversation going and focus on inclusion.** The very act of talking about inclusion will help it to become a reality. Promote diverse ideas and employee perspectives to emphasise how important inclusion is to the company culture, values and beliefs of the company. Think about how you communicate the concept of inclusion to new starters and how you make sure that the culture really does help advance the behaviour you want to see. Inclusive behaviour needs nurturing, particularly in a sales environment which can be highly stressful and competitive. Keep your staff on track by checking in with them (at all levels) and asking the right questions to make sure that open communication is practiced, diversity is valued and they feel motivated and engaged.

Chapter 7

Accountability and Responsibility

Your new recruit

Activity and accountability must be transparent, particularly for a new starter. Regardless of whether people are working in the same location or remotely, letting salespeople know what everyone else is doing is important for holding people to account. Your CRM is a crucial factor in communicating and recording activity and effort; your sales team must be diligent in using it, if you expect them to lead by example.

Maintaining energy in the team, when they're working from home or remotely, is more difficult than when they're together in the office. It can have a demotivating impact on new recruits, especially if they're isolated and unable to build the relationships they need in their new workplace. Updating the CRM helps to address this from a customer information and who is doing what perspective, increasing the frequency of virtual team meetings will help with team building and togetherness. Manager support on a regular basis is important too, for the new recruit and for the existing team.

Think about what can be achieved physically and virtually to maintain energy, motivation and togetherness and get them in the diary.

Accountability is the key to measuring the achievement of your new starter. They should be keen to accept accountability and responsibility for their progress. When you plan their onboarding schedule, include timeframes for the milestones you've laid out for them. Set their first goal to match the minimum you'd expect from anyone in your sales team in a set period. Setting the bar too low will not motivate them to get up to speed quickly. Make sure they have the tools they need and are trained to use them. Training and upskilling needs should be revealed in the first month, allowing you to schedule them before the end of the plan. Your goal is to get a return on your investment as quickly as possible, they should be aiming to be a fully functioning member of the sales team at the conclusion of the onboarding period.

Responsibility goes hand in hand with accountability and taking responsibility for getting up to speed should be emphasised and excuses not accepted. You have invested in them and you are providing every reasonable help with their learning, training and development to ensure they are functioning effectively as part of your sales team. They must be held accountable and responsible for their progress.

Is it fair and reasonable to expect this so early in their role?

This is a better question: 'is it fair not to?' To motivate and help your new sales person achieve their objectives, they must own it and it must matter if they fail. A new sales hire should relish the opportunity to prove their value to the team. You can help them to succeed by having a clear sales process and communicating clearly. Your process should be a logical, step by step roadmap of what you want, what you expect and how you want them to do it. Any well-run sales department will document clear working directives, set fair targets based on accurate forecasting and communicate them consistently to the sales team.

How to hold people to account and maintain standards

The first step is to make sure the sales process in play is the best practice for your company and is communicated properly. Good communication is a two-way street, clearly spoken and confirmed understanding. You can only hold someone to account if they know what you expect and have the ability to deliver. They are accountable but you share the responsibility for making sure they have the tools. There is a saying that good people often leave good jobs because of a bad boss, this can also refer to a bad sales manager who wants to be the king pin and fails to give the team what they need.

In a high achieving sales team, each person wants accountability for their performance, because it equates to achieving personal targets and contributes to team targets, which should be linked to their commission and bonus payments.

While your new starter is working through their onboarding plan, emphasising the benefit of being accountable for their performance will start them in good working habits. The easiest, quickest and most cost-effective way to be sure they're in tune with your existing sales team is to give them access to your sales playbook. A sales playbook is your documented sales process. If you don't have anything documented, you need to create it otherwise you're delaying your new starter's progress and risk them settling into bad habits or behaviour inconsistent with your company values.

If you were a sports coach with a new player, you'd hand them the playbook containing all the plays the team uses and expect the new player to learn them, practice them and follow each play to make sure they didn't let the team down.

Their role would be clearly laid out, consistent performance would be expected and success anticipated, with clear consequences for failure. Your sales team shouldn't be any different. Maintaining this sporting analogy, if you're the Manager, you typically also assume the role of the coach. Every team member benefits from being coached and supported. It's during training, coaching and practice that good habits are learned, skills are refreshed and your team is motivated to excel. Coaching and one-to-one mentoring quickly illuminates shortcomings and allows you, as the coach, to make decisions that ensure anyone not being responsible for their actions on sales targets, is held to account. When a team sees that it matters what they as individuals achieve and that underachievers are called out, they will feel valued and see how they contribute to the overall success.

A simple rule: Don't skip sales meetings

You may have a fire to put out, but learning the difference between urgent and important can be the key to motivating your team to success or letting them drift into failure. A skipped meeting or one-to-one tells the sales person they are not important. Sometimes things happen that are unavoidable so think around the problem and how you can do both. If you're the sales manager and need to attend a big deal meeting, take the rookie with you as a shadowing event. It's a good way to train them and show best practice in action. Include a briefing talk in the car and a debrief after the event.

Short daily meetings

Daily Huddles or regular get togethers, online or in person, can be a great way to get everyone to contribute, even your new starters. This is a less formal communication and is able to build relationships more quickly and encourage collaboration. Frequency is the key to smashing the barriers between old and new salespeople, helping underachievers to learn from top performers in a less competitive environment.

I've found that the majority of salespeople hate roleplay, finding it intimidating and not wanting to look silly. However, it's essential to know what your salespeople are actually saying to prospects and how they're saying it. Roleplay is a great way to do this. One of the best is the 3-way pitch. One person is the customer, one is the sales person and one is the observer. Give them an example and let them each talk for a minute. The sales person pitches, the customer responds and the observer reports. Rotate the roles so each player has a go at each discipline. It's a great way to get actual experiences out in the open and can be done face to face or online with minimal preparation.

Regular Meetings – weekly and monthly

To maintain standards, more formal sales team meetings should be held regularly with participation required from all members of the sales team, new recruits included. The agenda should be standard each time and team members expected to participate and supply real information in the form of numbers, reports and case studies. Included should be:

- Company update by sales manager
- Review of the success (or not) of lead generation,
- Conversion rates
- Road blocks
- Deal reviews
- Health check for new recruits
- Health check for salespeople
- An element of training or knowledge sharing
- Resolution of actions from the last meeting
- Actions to be delivered by the next meeting

Deal reviews, both successful and unsuccessful should be reviewed as a team. If your sales team's culture is overly competitive, accepting accountability for a failed deal can be problematic. It's important to create a no-blame culture, to make sure all deal reviews are analysed and used as a learning and collaboration tool for the whole team. They will learn as much from a failure as they will from a success. Taking responsibility for failure is important to a sales person's growth. The painful lesson of losing a sale is remembered longer than a quick success.

The Sales Manager

Sales management is one of the toughest jobs in any business, not least because the sales manager is accountable to senior management for the success of the sales team and accountable to the team, making sure they have the tools and training to achieve sales targets.

Managing a sales team requires specific skill and training. Promoting your best sales person to sales manager can backfire spectacularly. Removing your best seller and expecting them to exhibit the entirely different skills required to motivate and manage a team is a big ask. The sales manager doesn't need to be your best sales person, but they should be able to inspire the team and walk the walk. Their job is to focus on improving the team, in terms of quality and quantity. To earn the trust and respect of the team, the sales manager should have significant sales experience. Mental toughness is required and respected, especially in a competitive environment. All salespeople have to accept rejection as part of their daily work and they need to know the sales manager has the same mental strength and resilience, or they won't accept their leadership.

I think the most common sales promotion mistake in the book is the promotion of the top sales person into the sales manager role. I've lost count of the number of times I've seen a good sales person drafted into the role of sales manager purely by virtue of their sales tally. I'm sure there are examples of this working, but they are in the minority. The sales person knows what the customer wants and knows how to do it, but that doesn't go anywhere near what's needed to be a good sales manager. A highly performing sales person requires a huge shift in mindset to be able to manage a team of salespeople. Worse still is when they're also expected to carry their same quota before they were elevated to Manager, it's often a recipe for disaster. What makes this story especially sad, is that when the promotion fails, as it often does, the sales person feels they have failed. It's a very public failure for them and usually they're not able to return to their former sales only role and they end up leaving the business to save face. Nobody wins in this scenario; in fact, it often does a lot of damage to the team's morale in addition to burning the top achiever.

As I said, my view is that the sales manager's primary objective, is to grow the sales team, in terms of quality and quantity.

Uncomfortable conversations

Uncomfortable conversations should be tackled immediately. Approaching difficult situations with the whole team present, help to ease the tension and invites the team to move on and seek solutions. These conversations may be awkward and not what the team wants, but transparent communication and being part of the solution, will help to stabilise the team and dispel any negativity. Ignoring shortcomings and not addressing them, will clearly send the message to your salespeople that you don't think it matters. It does matter. Negativity is quick to grow and will spread through the team. Even a tough solution that might send a shockwave through the team, will have less impact if delivered as soon as the challenge arises.

Helping the sales team without micro-managing

Getting the best out of the sales team means communicating clearly, asking for feedback and removing as many roadblocks as possible. This might be providing training when you see a lack of skill, practice sessions and role play to get them comfortable with customer interactions e.g. handling objections.

Check the make-up of your team

Is your sales structure right for the future?

Tasks and Responsibilities	Lead Generation	Internal Sales	Sales Executive	Key Accounts	Sales Manager	Sales Director
Develop a list of Prospects	✓	✓	✓			
Make Proactive New Sales Calls (phone)	✓	✓	✓			
Maintain clean data on CRM	✓	✓	✓	✓		
Liaise with Marketing on Campaigns	✓	✓	✓	✓	✓	
Book Sales Appointments	✓	✓	✓	✓		
Negotiating Prices with Customers		✓	✓	✓	✓	✓
Creating Proposals for Customers		✓	✓	✓	✓	
Quote Prices and Close Sales		✓	✓	✓	✓	✓
Provide Accurate Sales Forecasts		✓	✓	✓	✓	
Accountable for Individual Performance		✓	✓	✓	✓	✓
Liaising with Suppliers/Delivery	✓		✓	✓	✓	✓
Attend Sales Calls (person)			✓	✓	✓	✓
Embody Company Culture and Standards	✓	✓	✓	✓	✓	✓
Stay abreast of Sales and Industry Trends	✓	✓	✓	✓	✓	✓
Responsible for Growth of Key Accounts				✓		✓
Coordinating Sales Training					✓	
Managing Teams Day to Day Performance					✓	
Coach and Develop Direct Reports					✓	✓
Implement Sales Team Plans					✓	✓
Develop the Sales strategy for the business						✓
Take Ownership of the Total Sales Targets						✓
Set and implement the Sales Culture						✓

The make-up of your team needs to suit the type of sales you're making. Are your people 'start to finishers' or experts doing their own component of a multi faceted complex deal? A 'start to finisher' is traditionally a faster, straightforward sale. One sales person makes the initial contact, sets their own appointments, pitches and closes, possibly all in one meeting. A multi-faceted sale is a longer proposition with many moving parts. The deal will need multiple people and experts with specific, specialist knowledge. A team sales effort will be required to close the sale, which may take months, even years. The sales person might need to assume a more project management role to ensure all the moving parts work towards a successful conclusion.

Just like a sports team requires different types of players to ensure the team is equipped to compete, specialist salespeople are needed for different roles in the team. The sales manager must make sure the sales roles match the products and services the team is selling.

The sales tools

Technological sales tools remove the burden of slower, manual processes. It frees the team to do what they do best: sell. To be fully effective the sales manager must conduct regular reviews to make sure the team are using the tools to maximum advantage. Encouraging feedback will flag up anything that doesn't work or show what they need. If the tools need updating, it's important to schedule training sessions for the sales team and assess their proficiency after implementation.

Is the accountability one way only?

In addition to their accountability to management, a smart sales manager knows they are also accountable to the team. Setting clear expectations and achievable targets benefits both team and management. Regular check-ins up the line will reassure management that the sales team is functioning successfully. Down the line, they will offer visible support, provide clear communication and be an early warning if and when a team member is failing. Support with training and upskilling can rescue an underperformer if caught early, before too much damage to growth and profitability has occurred.

Reward and recognition and their part in seeing accountability as a good thing

If there are clearly communicated expectations, with properly forecasted targets, the sales team should feel confident about meeting or exceeding their objectives. When each team member is accountable for success with individual and team goals, their accountability should be linked to reward and recognition. Reward for achieving individual goals is motivational and personal in a way that achieving team goals isn't. Recognition of a job well done or a target achieved is fundamental for a person to feel valued and valuable. Credit for a good result should be given as freely as criticism and remedial training after a failure.

Sales targets are not optional, they must be achieved. The sales manager must lead their team and motivate them especially if external events interrupt the sales cycle. Sink or swim, the team must know that the sales manager will speak for them. In difficult times the sales manager must shoulder the responsibility for underachievement and in good times, give the team the credit for great results. If they fail to do this, the team will feel unappreciated and undervalued. Once the trust is gone and motivation is lost there will be no accountability and it will be much harder for sales targets to be reached.

How much accountability should the CEO assume?

It's tempting to say all of it, but it's dependent on the size, make up and hierarchy of the company. A good CEO will feel accountable and build a team of experts to deliver the results the company wants. In this scenario, the CEO's responsibility is primarily to appoint effective heads of department.

By the time a person reaches the position of CEO, whether they were an external appointment, founded the company, inherited it or rose through the ranks, they usually have similar strengths:

- Strategic thinking
- Ambition
- Vision
- Confidence

Without these, it's unlikely they'd have made it to CEO. Those strengths lead to finding these critically important things easy:

- Making decisions
- Building relationships
- Delivering results
- Adapting to external disruption
- Seeing the big picture

Steering a company to success requires the ability to be hands off and not in the thick of it. This suggests that the CEO is able to shift the accountability to the people appointed to do the work. This is very far from the truth. Being hands off doesn't mean uninvolved. The CEO is ultimately responsible and accountable for the success or failure of every part of the business which means growth, profit, company culture and the staff.

They must communicate the direction they want the business to take, setting and planning strategic long-term goals and have ultimate accountability to all the stakeholders who will include some or all of these:

- Management team
- Shareholders
- Investors
- All employees and contractors

- Suppliers
- Customers

Unlike most other employees in the company, the CEO isn't under the threat of termination. Their motivation is the success of the company and the carrot and the stick are just opposite sides of the same coin for them.

Who carries the can?

The sales manager owns the sales target, but ultimately, the CEO carries the can. The CEO sets the bar for leadership and integrity, which will cascade down through the layers of management and staff.

Good leaders are mindful of behaving with integrity, even when what they do isn't under scrutiny. Part of this should be inviting feedback from all levels and open communication up and down the organisation. Listening to feedback is not always comfortable and acting on it, to ensure there is continuous improvement, is even harder.

A culture where feedback is expected and encouraged will quickly lead to shared accountability. In a forum where everyone's view is respected and appreciated and feedback is discussed and acted upon, accountability becomes shared. Decisions feel democratic with ideas discussed and agreed. The responsibility stays with the CEO but the group participate in sharing the success or failure. A good definition of teamwork.

Chapter 8

The importance of process

The all-important sales process. Even now, when it's universally recognised that a documented sales process is essential to create an effective sales function, many businesses still think it'll take too much time or effort and just wing it. This is not headline news, but it should be. Having an overarching business vision and taking the time to provide an organisational framework, specifically for your sales processes, helps you optimise your sales opportunities, motivate and engage your sales staff and measure their progress towards achieving your company targets.

While your company vision shows what you want your company to be and achieve in the long term, your sales vision, provides structure and inspiration to your sales team. It links your overarching goals, to your sales-specific targets, acting as a GPS to get you from where you are, to where you want to be.

If you don't have any process in place, deconstruct the sales process of your most successful team members and use what they're doing as your starting point. Once you have a draft process, analyse it to see if there are any unnecessary steps. Change the process if you see you're losing business consistently at any stage.

I'm not suggesting that you stamp out individuality in your sales team or create a team of clones. I am suggesting, that devising a consistent sales process will keep your team consistent and improve your overall results, adding a winning formula to their individual talent and personality. Look at every part of your process to maximise opportunities and review your qualification criteria regularly to make sure they're effective and suited to your products and your customers.

If you want to set up your sales structure to support your sales team, but you don't have time, you should consider engaging an external advisor to do it for you. It can be a good solution if you have time constraints, with no baggage or sales targets to distract them. Your external advisor will be totally focused on building your consistent and sustainable sales system, in consultation with your management and sales team.

When your sales process is in place and you're seeing consistent results, remember to review it regularly for continuous improvement. Get your sales team involved in the review process. They're in the best position to see any market changes or external factors that will have an impact on your success. Consistency depends on great qualification, with a focus on leads with the greatest potential.

A regularly reviewed sales process, properly set targets and a sales team with KPIs to reward the behaviour you want to see, will keep your salespeople efficient, consistent and on track to achieve the results you want.

Keeping the new hire on track

The term back to basics is used to reference pretty much anything worth doing properly. It really means a refresher, with a check to clarify that skills have actually been learned in the first place. If you want your new starter to succeed, it's important for them to understand what you mean by 'sales skills'.

 Role play, listening to calls and shadowing senior members of your team during their onboarding journey will make sure there's no misunderstanding. Ensure there are timings and measurements in their 90-day plan with regular assessment and open communication to keep them on track. Schedule regular feedback time and share your evaluation of how they're doing. It gives you the opportunity to assess their progress and allows them to tell you what they need. These sessions will show how well, or not, they're fitting into the team and your company.

Regular one-to-one communication during their onboarding, highlights problems with skill set, mindset or training. Early warning of any problems and gives you the opportunity to fix them, or pull the plug, if it shows your new hire isn't a good fit with your team.

The basic sales skills

The following items are just the start of a long list of sales skills. Your industry, the size of your company, your products and a huge number of other variants will determine which are most important for you. Sales skills include:

- How to listen
- How to talk
- How to qualify
- How to understand behaviour
- How to network
- How to close
- How to handle objections

78

Your new starter must have the essential skills listed in your job description, but you also want them to bring their own individual style to the team. You don't want a team of clones. If your salespeople are encouraged to develop their own style, while following your consistent sales process, they'll appeal to your customers as genuine and trustworthy, not just a sales person looking for a win. Show your new starter you value what they bring to the team at the onboarding stage, because it builds confidence and helps build a solid foundation for success. A confident new starter who feels part of a supportive team will be motivated to achieve great results as quickly as possible.

The basics of the sales function

Your sales function is dependent on your industry and your company, but most sales functions need the following items, properly documented and followed, to achieve consistent, sustainable results. They are:

Products and Pricing – being an expert

Your new starter should have some idea of your products and services before they start, but by the end of their onboarding journey, they must know them inside out and back to front. They must understand and be able to articulate the value proposition for each one, know the current pricing strategy and understand your policy on discounts and margins. These are vital to make sure your products and services are not given away and will protect your integrity at the negotiation stage.

Qualification – knowing they are expected to apply your consistent, process every time

They must understand the importance of qualifying every lead, whether it's from a cold call or a referral, is not negotiable. Right from the first day, your new hire needs to be told that wasting time and money on unqualified leads will not be tolerated.

The importance of quality and constant qualification should never be underestimated. If done poorly (or not at all) it can be one of the largest unnoticed costs in running a sales team. If the answer is going to be 'No' then they must learn to get it as quickly as possible and move on.

Time and resources spent on leads with no intention of buying will soak up the working week and leave no time to sell to a properly qualified customer who is ready to buy. It must be clear that their target is not following leads, their target is to make sales.

Target Customers – recognising an ideal prospect who fits your buyer persona

Your new hire needs to be fully versed in who is most likely to buy your products or services. Give them all the information you have on your ideal prospect, your buyer persona based on what characteristics your best past and current customers share. They might include: industry, sector, location, age, education. Encourage your new starter to add to the buyer persona, if they discover any additional characteristic that will help win sales.

You must give clear and constant direction on who your target customers are, or they risk falling for the 'anyone and everyone' can buy what we're selling.

Competition – knowing who they are, how they sell and their weaknesses

Give your new hire a crash course in who your competitors are and if you have specific strategies to beat them. Include their different value propositions and examples of how to handle objections your prospects might raise with specific reference to your close competition.

Ensure that they know that your biggest competitor is the prospect who does nothing. A great way to help them understand the true importance of this (and improve your qualification), is to get them to ask, 'What will happen if nothing changes?' When they can see that, if there is no major impact, nothing will change, they will understand that they have a far less serious prospect.

Value Proposition – understanding what makes your company unique and the compelling reason your customers buy from you

Your value proposition might be: price, innovation, customer service, quality, environmental factors, locale, style or any other thing that differentiates you from your competition. You might have different value propositions for different products and services. If your new hire is to be successful, they must have a good understanding of your value propositions, as a company and for each product.

They must be able to articulate the value proposition when speaking to customers. If they over complicate it or it takes too long, they will not be clear. As Einstein said: 'If you can't explain it simply, you probably don't understand it well enough.'

Keeping the team consistent, efficient and on track

After the 90-day onboarding plan is completed, it's worth continuing with a looser monitoring schedule for the next six to nine months, or until your new starter's next regular development review. Keeping them motivated and on track is essential, once their onboarding is officially over.

Salespeople are not born with a mysterious ability to sell and, just like your new starter, they have been taught skills and techniques. Great salespeople, like great sports people, practice their skills to ensure they're at the top of their game. Whenever I meet salespeople who are apathetic or reluctant to practice their selling skills, an alarm bell rings. I read that reluctance as a demonstration of a closed mindset and a person limited in their plans or beliefs.

There's a lot more to sales success than the classic team of shiny-shoed salespeople sell, sell, selling. The days of a sales person cruising around the country, going from call to call has long gone. These people were often doing nothing more than a milk round of keeping in touch. If you have a sales person in your team who fits this description you should know that it's dangerous because:

- It breeds complacency with your customers (at risk of being under serviced and poached)
- Laziness with targets (ticking boxes for customer contacts, not bothering to sell)
- Lack of account developments 'stale conversations' (not working to produce opportunities to up and cross sell)
- Limited centralised data capture (not contributing new and useful data to create opportunities)

This type of sales person often thinks the customer is theirs. A new starter will quickly observe this type of behaviour and may assume it's part of the company's accepted practice. It's your responsibility to make the best use of every sales person, their skills, their knowledge and their relationships and be clear that customers belong to the business, not any individual sales person.

When a sales person in your team adds little or no value to your customers, especially if they are repeat online or remote buyers, you might need to find a better way of working. This might be through technology and automation without the stress of running a sales team and their egos at all.

Structure and good management, taking the pain out of sales

Every company has a responsibility to ensure that their salespeople are equipped with the best opportunity, to win the most deals, with the least effort. Most sales team environments are competitive and most sales leaders encourage competitive behaviour. It's healthy, it's motivating and keeps the team moving forward to achieve better results.

Setting realistic expectations and goals for your sales team is essential. Targets must be attainable and based on actual sales figures. External factors, such as movements in your industry and other market influences must be considered and targets adjusted if necessary. This will ensure you're not asking your team to do the impossible. Your management team is responsible for the clear communication of sales targets and outlining the consequences of failing to meet them. If you don't tell your team what you expect of them, you shouldn't be surprised if they fail to deliver it.

When you have clearly stated your expectations, it's vital that you don't accept it if they fall short of properly set targets. This is about accountability and responsibility. Your team must be held to account and accept the responsibility and the consequences of failure. This might be the withholding of bonuses or other incentives. If you let them off the hook, you are contributing to the likelihood of future weak results and targets not met. Good management requires you to take responsibility for delivering tough messages when they're needed and holding the team to account. When you have a good structure in place and realistic targets, poor performance should not be accepted.

A great tip I learned a while ago

To maintain focus, look at every opportunity and know three things:

- The number (value)
- The date (typically the expected close date)
- The consequence (things that may or may not happen)

Good management is a complex mixture. Your relationship with your team can be the key to their success and on the flip side, the reason for their failure. Your team must feel you value them and by giving them responsibility to achieve their targets and holding them accountable, you are showing them that you believe in them.

It is your responsibility to keep to the planned activities that are important to your team and deliver what you have promised. Cancelling team meetings or scheduled one-to-ones to tackle something more 'urgent', will set a dangerous precedent. There is no room for poor time management in any part of the sales function. Proactive planning, clear communication and good delegation of responsibilities, will help to prevent any urgent interruptions. Postponing meetings will simply convey to the team that they are not important.

Be a good leader

There are many things that make a good leader. Personality, style and how well you communicate. Overall, good leaders have a few things in common:

- Express what they expect clearly
- Provide the proper tools and coaching for success
- Their actions show they have confidence in the team's ability
- Take responsibility, up the line, when results are bad
- Give credit to the team, up the line, when results are good
- Demand the excellence they demonstrate
- Be able to admit it when they are wrong

Managing a sales team or running a company is an exciting, dynamic and rewarding position and one to be taken seriously. A good team should keep you on your toes and demand you be the leader they deserve as they strive to exceed their targets.

As the leader you are part of the team. Be available, be accountable and hold them to account, communicate clearly and often and celebrate every success.

Chapter 9

Why Leadership Matters

The sales team is at the pointy end in most businesses and whoever assumes the leadership role, is under constant pressure to achieve the sales targets and improve company growth. The sales manager is expected to lead by example, motivate the troops, create the sales strategy, analyse results and any other number of tasks. The leader may have been 'volunteered' for the role and it may be in addition to their real job of CEO, CFO, General Manager or sometimes the most senior or successful sales person. They haven't been selected because they have the diverse range of skills needed to lead a sales team. It's a tough ask for any of these people, skilled at their real job, now expected to have the full set of strategic, diplomatic, sales and people skills needed to be successful.

Statistics indicate that sales leaders take 9-10 months to become effective in a new role and, on average, stay in a position for less than two years. This is not financially healthy for either the sales leader or the company who employs them and is often the reason that the job is done away with and amalgamated with another senior role. The job is difficult to fill, precisely because of the range of diverse skills required and the attitude and effort needed to do it well.

Winston Churchill summed it up perfectly when he said: 'Continuous effort, not strength or intelligence, is the key to unlocking our potential.'

A successful sales manager will:

- Recognise early that success isn't only about knowledge or position, it's about being consistent and continuing to grow as you apply your knowledge
- Be able to influence their team to embody the values and beliefs of the company
- Find out what the team needs to be successful and make sure they have it
- Be clear about the definition of success and will make sure the team knows and understands it
- Control their own destiny by having the courage to face issues and challenges
- Won't be afraid to ask for input from the team and knows the best teams are those that feel valued for their contribution
- Lead with a light hand and won't hinder the natural ability of their salespeople by micromanaging them

- Ensure they know what the team needs to do, how to do it and create a sales plan and strategy to set them up for success
- Never forget they are part of the team and behave accountably and responsibly
- Make tough decisions swiftly after considering all options
- Communicate clearly with all key stakeholders: the team, senior management and customers and understand the value of good communication in leadership and success
- Remember to keep going, continuing to learn and improve
- Be confident and understand it's not a sign of weakness to acknowledge a wrong decision or ask for feedback from the team
- Encourage the team to share their knowledge for everyone to benefit
- Understand the value of good communication and how they are perceived by the team
- Value a good relationship with every individual sales person and use the words 'Good job' and 'Well done'

There is no one way to be a good leader, there isn't a one size fits all because we're all very different. Some people have natural leadership ability and take it easily in their stride, others struggle with it every day. The odd thing is, it's not always possible to guess which is which. You might think your team leader finds it easy, but they may feel they struggle with it.

It's complex, rewarding, thankless, frustrating, overwhelming and tiring. Putting all the factors in place should bring success, but sometimes it doesn't.

Often the employing business is more responsible for failed sales hires than the individuals themselves. It is the company's responsibility to provide satisfactory sales leadership. Without proper leadership, you're likely to have insufficient training and poor onboarding. There are plenty of examples of great leaders, with the ability to get a team of average performers, to achieve greater results than each individual could have achieved on their own.

Ultimately, enjoying being a leader is the thing that matters. Confidence and enjoyment are contagious. When you enjoy what you do and face each challenge confidently, you stand the best chance of success.

Relationships Matter

We've all had the phony relationship experience with a sales person who plays the friendship game to get the sale. We know it's fake, but we fall for it anyway because hope triumphs over experience. Feeling let down after the sale is the result and a reluctance to trust a sales person again, but we do.

Relationship building is tough unless you know the rules. Except, there are no rules and that's part of the problem. Nothing is either right or wrong, it's all subjective. What works with one person won't work with another. The good news is, we are social beings who like to interact. Nothing fails all the time, nothing works all the time, but some things work some of the time.

Where to begin

Start with what makes you comfortable. You are unlikely to appear genuine if you try to mimic someone else's go to method. Building a successful relationship needs a few basics:

- Integrity, you must be genuine
- Empathy, be aware of the effect you're having
- Alertness, watch for body language and defensive answers
- Emotional intelligence, understand the impact you might have both physically and verbally

Ideas to help you find your style

- Think about the best conversation you've had with a stranger and analyse why it worked
- Pull out appropriate things and decide if you could use them with a customer
- Prepare safe, fall-back questions to deploy, if you sense the customer is not responding to your line of conversation
- Don't be afraid to change tack if you don't make any headway, your goal is to sell, not to make a friend, so switch to a transactional approach if you need to

What should relationships look like?

Relationships should be easy. They should be stress-free, enjoyable and each party should know exactly where they stand and be respectful of differing opinions.

Equality, integrity and co-operation are vital elements in any successful long-term relationship.

The Manager and the sales person

There is an immediate disconnect in this relationship because the sales person is not equal in work status to the manager. If one of the key markers for a successful relationship is equality, how will it be possible to overcome this fundamental stumbling block? That's the dilemma and also why there are no rules because each situation needs to work around the outrageous stumbling blocks to create a great working relationship.

Not equal in status, doesn't mean not equal as people. The manager and the sales person are equal in terms of everything that matters because the relationship must be based on things outside the construct of organisational requirements. Building a relationship must exist outside the reason for the relationship. It's a paradox in that without the workplace the two people might not meet and have a relationship, but although they have met in the workplace, their relative positions in the workplace can't be the basis of the relationship if it's to have any value. Stepping outside the status, the manager and sales person must relate as two individuals. If we look again at the basics:

- Integrity, you must be genuine
- Empathy, be aware of the effect you're having
- Alertness, watch for body language and defensive answers
- Emotional intelligence, understand the impact you might have both physically and verbally

And consider two scenarios it will illustrate this point more clearly.

Scenario A
Manager Smith meets new sales hire Jones on Jones' first day at work.

> **Smith**: Welcome to the company, great to have you on board. You'll be working at that desk. I run this team. We're a friendly, tight knit bunch but don't take advantage, you're here to do a job of work and this is a competitive environment. I expect great things from you, my door is always open but I don't expect to see you every five minutes, got it? We value hard work and independence, best way to learn is to just get on with it. Any questions?

Jones: No, thanks, looking forward to getting started. Thanks for...
>   *Phone rings*
Smith: Yes, hello – great, hoping you'd ...
>   *Waves his hand to signal Jones to leave*

Manager Smith shows by his manner that he doesn't consider Smith to be his equal as a person. The words support the feeling of higher status, but it's the manner in addition to the words that matters.

Scenario B
Manager Smith meets new sales hire Jones on Jones' first day at work.

> **Smith**: I'm **Smith**, welcome to the company **Jones**, it's great to have you on board. You'll be working at that desk. **As you know**, I run this team. We're a friendly, tight knit bunch **and they're all keen to get to know you. I'm not sure how much I can tell you at this point, you should be warned that this is a competitive environment** but I expect great things from you. My door is always open but I don't I don't expect you to need much help. We value hard work and independence. **I think** the best way to learn, is just get on with it. **That's enough from me for now, do you** have any questions?

> **Jones**: No, thanks, looking forward to getting started. Thanks for.
> >   *Phone rings*
> **Smith**: Sorry Jones, do you mind? Take a seat, I won't be a minute.
> >   *Waves his hand to signal Jones to sit down*

The inclusion of a few words changes the message. New hire Jones is under no illusion about Smith's status but because Smith shares the information with feeling or opinion phrases like: 'I'm not sure/you should be warned/that's enough from me', Smith is reaching beyond the superior status to speak to the new hire as an equal. When the phone rings, acknowledging Jones with: 'sorry Jones, do you mind?' confirms this. In reality Jones is unlikely to object, but the polite gesture makes Jones feel of value to the manager. These small but crucial additions, jump the relationship ahead to introduce mutual respect, giving it a better chance of being productive. There's no doubt about the organisational status between the two. Smith's manner doesn't detract from the authority of the position, but it signals the type of behaviour expected by demonstrating courtesy and professionalism. This builds trust and loyalty and is the beginning of a mutually respectful working relationship.

The relationships between the sales manager and sales team members are the most important. To ensure the company will meet or exceed the sales targets, there must be mutual respect, trust, loyalty with all committed to the team.

The CEO, the Head of Sales, the Sales Leader and the Sales Manager

The relationship between the CEO and whoever has the responsibility to manage the sales team, must follow the same guidelines as the manager's relationship with the team:

- Integrity, each person must be genuine
- Empathy, being aware of the effect they're having
- Alertness, watching for body language and defensive answers
- Emotional intelligence, understanding the impact being made, physically and verbally

Creating a connection that supersedes status, is again the key to a productive relationship. The CEO must run the company to be the most successful it can be. The sales manager is part of the management team to make this happen. There has to be trust, loyalty and an ability to work together to ensure set objectives are achieved.

The CEO must empathise with the sales manager's tasks and must support the strategy outlined to meet the sales targets. If there is a genuine connection, over and above the reporting line, the CEO will be able to trust in the decisions made and the sales manager will be able to make good decisions, knowing the CEO will support them.

The Sales person and the customer

This relationship will flow down from how well relationships have been formed from the CEO, through the sales manager to the sales Team. Building a relationship, even in a simple one-off transaction, is important because a genuine desire to find a solution that works for a customer will lead to positive reviews (online), recommendations, repeat sales and the opportunity to up and cross sell. Once trust is established, closing the sale is easy and rewarding.

There are basic techniques, or you could call them common sense, that make relationship building easy.

How to impress a customer (win friends and influence people)

- Demonstrate value
- Find out what the customer needs by asking and listening
- Provide a solution that suits their needs and give other recommendations
- Handle their objections
- Only close the sale if it's a win/win
- Always do, what you said you were going to do
- After the sale, continue to add value

Demonstrating value

While you're establishing the relationship, asking general questions and listening attentively, show your knowledge and expertise by offering ideas and useful tips. It might be an introduction to another related supplier, a website they should look at or anything else that will help them.

Find out what they need by asking and listening

Ask targeted questions to ascertain their specific needs and keep listening and probing to make sure you can provide a solution that will help them and that they are ready to commit to buy. During this discovery phase it's important to begin preliminary qualification. You must determine that they are ready to buy, they demonstrate a need for your produce (or service) that they have the budget and you can supply it to meet their timeline.

However good the rapport with a customer, if they don't meet your qualification criteria, you must withdraw. This time. Building a relationship is a long-term strategy and a 'no' now, might not mean 'no' next time. Continue to demonstrate your knowledge and value, but park the sales pitch for now. If you've established a good relationship, you'll be able to pick it up at a more appropriate time when they're ready to buy and your qualification criteria are met. In the meantime, if they appreciate your acceptance of their current situation, they're likely to recommend you and welcome your advance down the track.

Provide a solution that suits their needs and give other recommendations

Once a prospect qualifies, you can start to use what you've discovered about your buyer to build a solution for them. Your product knowledge and suggestions will form the basis of what you deliver. Focus on the challenges that will be resolved best by the particular products or services you offer. Use your expertise to anticipate other needs you see now, or that from experience, you know will occur in the future.

Show your credentials by citing a key customer with a similar issue and how they benefited from your solution.

Handle their objections

You will always face objections in the selling process. It's a healthy and basic way for the customer to make sure they're not making a mistake. It's much better to have a question asked and answered satisfactorily, than to allow doubts to fester.

Objections should be seen as an opportunity to showcase exactly why your solution is perfect for your customer. A mindset that interprets 'it's too expensive' as 'persuade me that it's worth the money' will allow you to outline all the benefits, reinforce your value proposition and give you the opportunity to double check that it is the right solution for them clearly and calmly. Your reputation and your company's reputation are on the line. Listen to them and don't soft soap over the objection. If they're really having cold feet, be open and honest with them. Don't disregard their doubt, go back to basics if you have to and outline the solution again, but understand they might need time to absorb all the information.

Ask them what doubts they're having and continue to answer. It's vital to get to the stage where they know you understand what they're asking. Continue to ask questions until you're absolutely sure you're both talking about the same things.

Only close the sale if it's a win/win

Closing a sale is a cooperative exchange with your customer. They have a need; you have a product that fills their need. Simple!

Not always simple. Price, value, cost of implementation on top of purchase may all present stumbling blocks for your customer. Yes, they want it, no they want it cheaper, more comprehensively supported, any manner of other extras.

Negotiation can be fraught, but it doesn't have to be. After all, you and your customer want the same result, a successful sale/purchase.

Preparation will help you meet them on even ground to get that result. Know what concessions you can make without eroding your profit and think about extras that are easy to implement at minimal cost e.g. longer guarantee or extension of product support. Most importantly though, know your walk away point and stick to it. The sales must be within your strategic growth and profit range, a sale at any cost is not acceptable.

After the sale, continue to add value

Keep in touch with your customer once your solution has been delivered and implemented. Ask for referrals and write a case study highlighting each step of the process. Add them to your mailing list and diarise phone calls to check in. Add them to your LinkedIn contacts and follow them on social media. Congratulate them on significant milestones and make your company part of their success story.

Keep building the relationship and be there to suggest further solutions when you see an opportunity. If you've done a good job and your customer is happy, don't be afraid to ask them for referrals – they're FREE leads!

When I conduct a workshop, I always encourage the participants to ask their customers for referrals. Don't wait and hope or wait for the customer to think to do it, they might not ever think about it.

If you feel awkward or presumptuous, practice how to ask in a way that feels comfortable. I once concluded a meeting with a happy customer and walked out of their office with a good-sized order and six referrals. It was enough to keep me busy for the next month and the customer was delighted to do it, because he felt he'd had good service over and above his expectation. Personal experience has shown me time and time again, that passion for the job, can create a very happy win/win.

Chapter 10

Conclusions

Nothing beats good onboarding backed up with a proper structure and enthusiasm

After more than 30 years in business, mostly sales, I know from all sides of the equation that nothing, not one thing in the sales toolbox, beats good onboarding.

At the beginning of my sales journey, I was fortunate to have six weeks (unpaid) training to sell life insurance. It was in the 'old' days before the internet, but using basic computers. It was a grounding that was intense, repetitive, dull by today's standards but thorough. There was no opportunity to slack off because you couldn't progress to the next week, unless you passed what you'd learned that week. It taught me the value of structure, assessment and measurement.

As a Sales manager and a business owner, I've been in the position to hire and fire. I've interviewed to employ a hopeful candidate and I've been that hopeful candidate. I've been thrown in at the deep end and had to struggle to get the information I needed to survive, let alone succeed and I've instituted really good onboarding plans for my new starters.

In interviews, try not to do all the talking. It's crucial to let the sales person talk, they will reveal themselves and after all, it's their interview. I've held interviews before where I thought it was important to make them aware of how great an opportunity, I was giving them. I set about selling them on how great my business was. I realised much later that I'd only expected the interviewee to answer yes or no and make the occasional comment to agree with me. It was a great interview and I was the convinced the person should get the job. We were perfectly aligned, how could we not be, I barely let them speak!

Ask them an open-ended question and let them tell you about the great deals they've made. We all love to talk about our successes. Make sure you interject with questions about what went well and what they actually did in the process. In an effort to impress, it's easy to take credit for a team effort when you are one of many who achieved the goal.

This book has been about the value of good onboarding how it looks now and what it should be. I have absolutely no doubt that the poor statistics around sales hire are mostly to do with sub-standard onboarding.

Throughout my years of experience, I have observed that it is normal for most businesses to operate with no documented sales process, no recruitment strategy and onboarding that consists of pointing a new hire at a desk, giving them a logon and telling them to get started.

The statistics around sales hire failure would be astonishing if not for those three items. My advice is always:

- Recruit mindfully, with a strategy to hire the right candidate
- Put in place a good onboarding plan
- Give the new starter access to your documented sales playbook as quickly as possible

How personality helps, but ultimately doesn't matter

Personality versus experience and skills is something I think about a lot. We get into trouble when we hire people who interview well. A candidate with a compatible personality, who makes us feel comfortable is hard to resist, even if they don't have the skills and experience, we want. Ultimately, it doesn't matter if we like them or not, but good attitude is critical to ensure they are willing to do the job in the way we want it done.

I once interviewed a sales person for a client, who claimed at the top of their CV, that they had closed a £6m individual sale to BT. It was pretty impressive and having not sold a £6m deal to BT myself, I wanted to know more about the actual mechanics and process of the sale. Surprisingly, the guy started to back off and wanted to change the subject. I continued to probe, he changed the subject, I probed again and I gradually worked out that of the 12 meetings needed to close the deal, he was involved in only 7 of them. He hadn't sourced the lead in the first place, had to bring in a manager and then a director of his company for the final three meetings. It was a substantial and huge sale, he had been an integral part of it, but it was not an individual sale. In asking him to talk about it, he revealed a lot about his attitude and behaviour. The sale was still impressive, he wasn't.

How training and good attitude overcome most difficulties

Good attitude is the essential ingredient, regardless of skills, experience and personality. A good attitude will allow for ongoing training and a capacity to follow documented processes. Lack of experience or poor skills can be coached up to the standard required if the candidate has a ready and willing attitude.

When to throw in the towel and admit defeat

Perhaps one of the most difficult tasks a Sales manager faces is when to sack an employee, particularly a new hire. There is no quick right or wrong answer. Try to find the sweet spot in the process right between your sales team saying, 'what took you so long?' and 'whoa - that was a bit quick!' because when you decide to let someone go, it will have an impact on the rest of the team. You need to protect the overall morale of your team and make sure your sales performance doesn't suffer. If the perception is the dismissal is unfair then you might end up with more problems than those caused by the person staying in a role for which they were unsuited.

I must say, in over 30 years, I've rarely heard someone comment that a dismissal was a bit quick. Too many Managers put off making a difficult call, even when it's right, and then must reflect on why it took them so long.

Get out your checklist and tick off these items

- Did you make a good decision when you hired the person?
- Did you give them a structured onboarding with assessment and development?
- Are they failing because they need more training?
- Was training for the tools and technology to do the job part of their onboarding plan?
- Are they embracing your methodology?
- Are you coaching them and are they coachable?
- Have they had enough time and attention?
- Are they simply the wrong hire for the role?

When you know that you have done all you can, you must face the fact that you'll have to let them go and do it quickly.

Whatever the reason was for hiring them in the first place, an underperforming salesperson who has been properly coached, trained, given the tools and time to settle in, is obviously a poor fit. It may be with the company, the sales team or the product or service they are trying to sell. Keeping them once you made the decision is a disruptive influence on the whole team.

It's time to let them loose to find something better suited to their skills, somewhere else. The sooner the better because the longer you allow them to stay - the more they will damage your culture, your team, your bottom line, and your reputation.

Learning from your mistakes and celebrating success

Charles Darwin is misquoted as saying 'survival of the fittest' but he actually said:

'It is not the strongest of the species that survives, nor the most intelligent that survives. It is the one that is most adaptable to change.'

Our ability to form social groups for safety and our ability to adapt technologies has allowed us to evolve and thrive. Ability to adapt means learning from our mistakes and not repeating them. Having a dynamic sales process and a sales team with a good attitude will help any business adapt to the ever-changing business environment. As technology advances, buyer behaviour changes and external events dictate how we do business we need to be able to adapt more than ever before to help us navigate the next phase with confidence.

Celebrating success reinforces team spirit and shares the credit for it. Using the words 'well done' and 'good job' are motivating and every success celebrated, nurtures a positive culture. As the saying goes: Success breeds success and it does with research showing that each success leads to significant increases in subsequent rates of success.

As companies understand that good candidates look beyond the financial and want other cultural benefits when making their decision about their next employer, businesses should consider the advantages of promoting their onboarding plan and how it demonstrates their investment in the success of the candidate. A company that offers a structured training plan with a clear explanation as to the contribution of its people is seriously interested in their own growth, profit and success and values the part every employee plays in that success.

Thank you for reading

I love writing, speaking and learning about sales and I'd like to thank you for reading this book. It's always great to hear from people who have sought improvement and taken control of their sales function. As a lifelong learner myself, I'm always happy to connect directly or via LinkedIn:

https://www.linkedin.com/in/matt-garman-2807794/

Lightning Source UK Ltd.
Milton Keynes UK
UKHW020657221220
375698UK00006B/163